For Winter, who always asks me
about my day and listens on our walks
home from school. You once asked
if this book was for you,
and here's loving proof that it is.
—FG

THE ULTIMATE ART MUSEUM

FERREN GIPSON

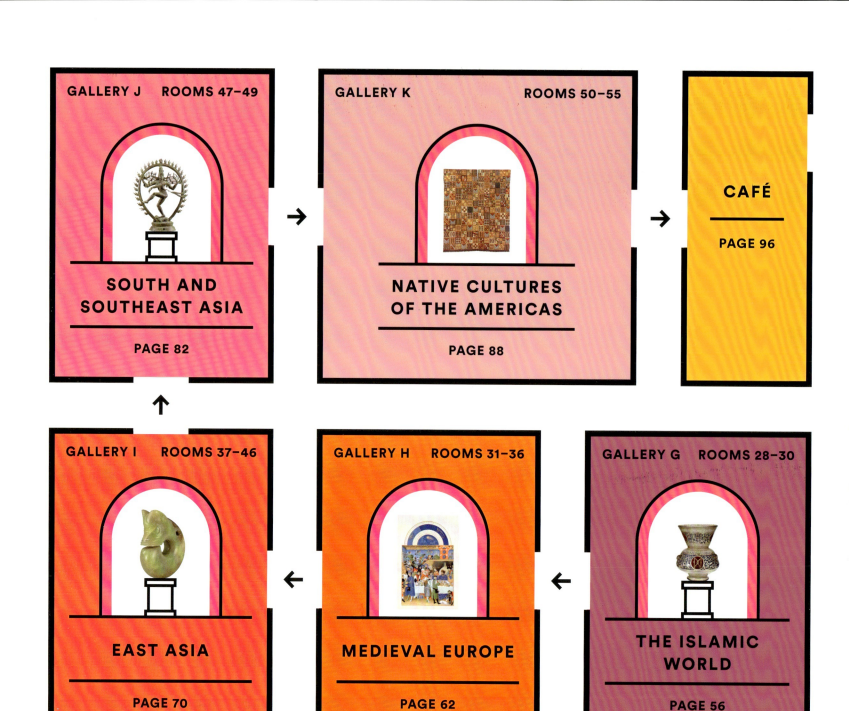

GALLERY J	ROOMS 47–49

SOUTH AND SOUTHEAST ASIA

PAGE 82

GALLERY K	ROOMS 50–55

NATIVE CULTURES OF THE AMERICAS

PAGE 88

CAFÉ

PAGE 96

GALLERY I	ROOMS 37–46

EAST ASIA

PAGE 70

GALLERY H	ROOMS 31–36

MEDIEVAL EUROPE

PAGE 62

GALLERY G	ROOMS 28–30

THE ISLAMIC WORLD

PAGE 56

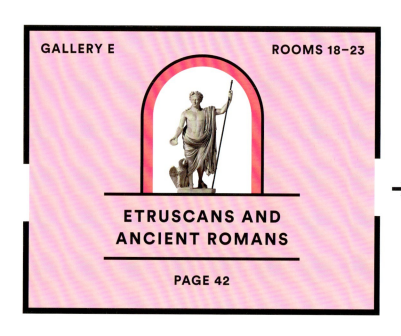

GALLERY E	ROOMS 18–23

ETRUSCANS AND ANCIENT ROMANS

PAGE 42

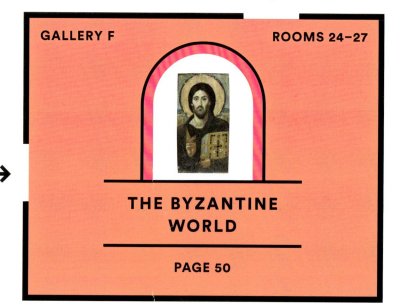

GALLERY F	ROOMS 24–27

THE BYZANTINE WORLD

PAGE 50

Museum Map

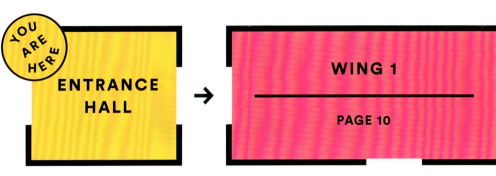

Our museum is so enormous that it's divided into three wings, each with color-coded galleries and rooms.

Wings are grouped by time periods, starting with art that is 40,000 years old in wing one. From there we move forward through time to the end of wing three, with artists who are still working today! Each of the galleries and rooms explores interesting themes, places, people, and ideas across the ages.

Feel free to run around and jump from one wing, gallery, or room to another. No one will stop you! And you'll always have this map to tell you where you are if you get lost.

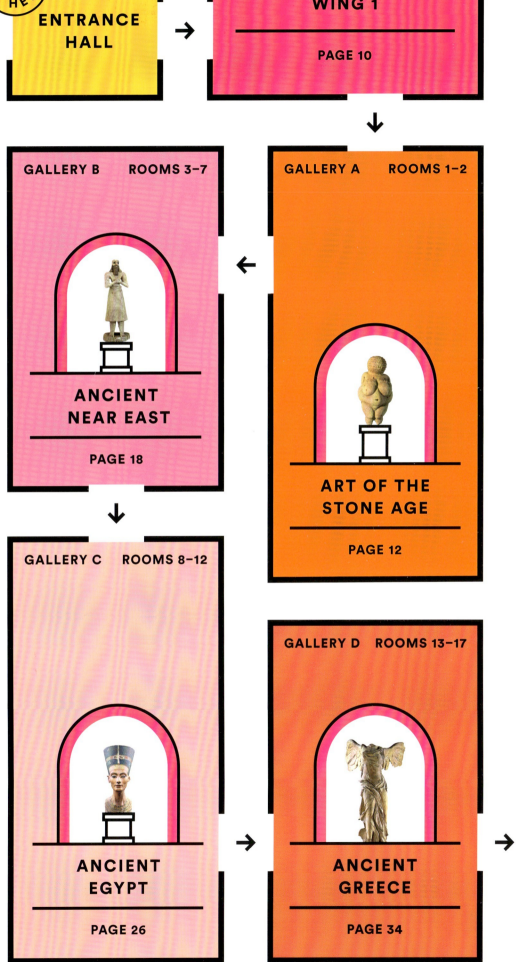

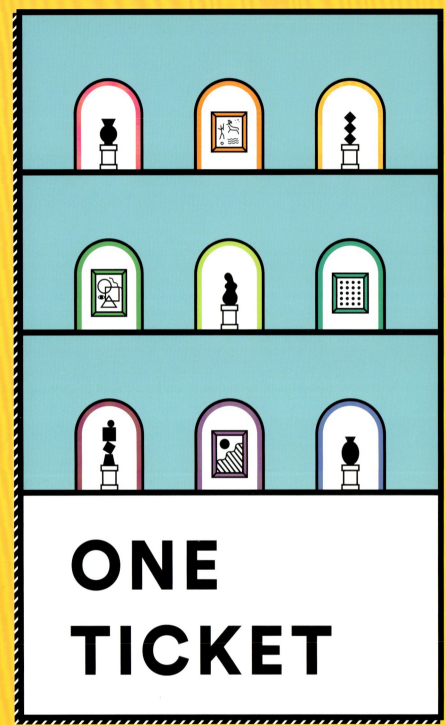

Welcome to the most magnificent museum in the world!

Take a stroll down our winding corridors, and wander through rooms filled with art throughout the ages!

 HERE WE GO!

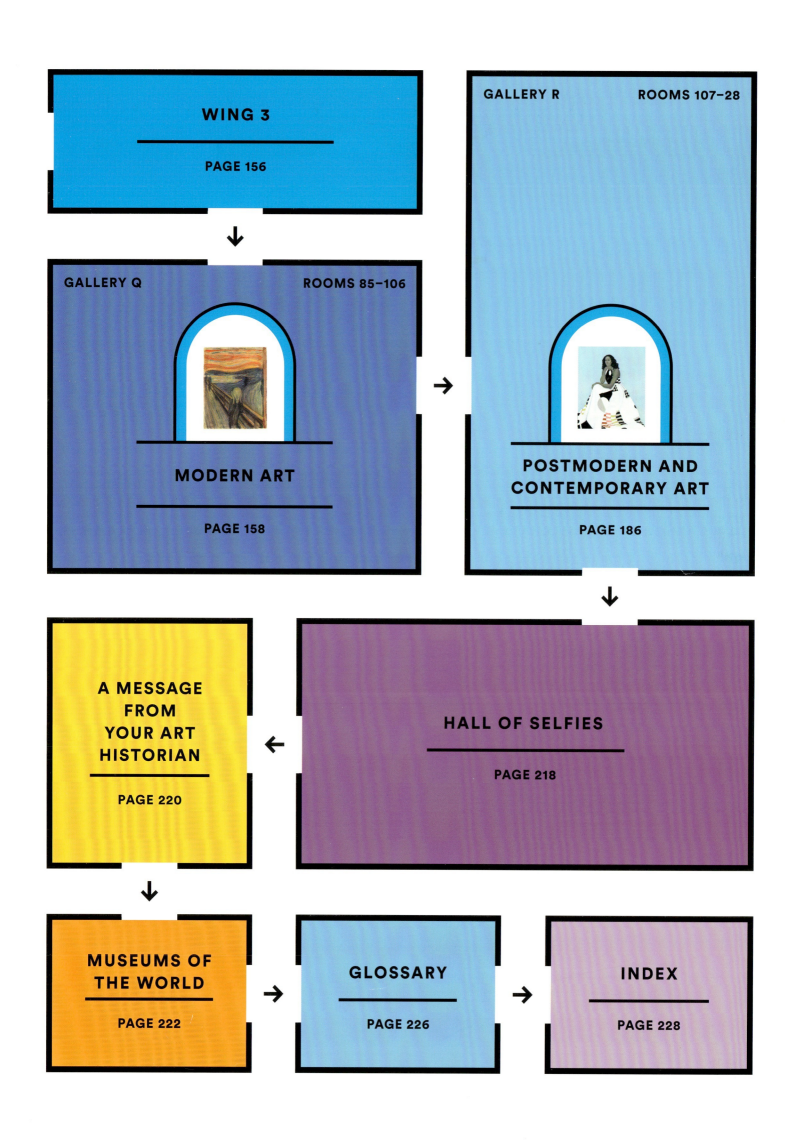

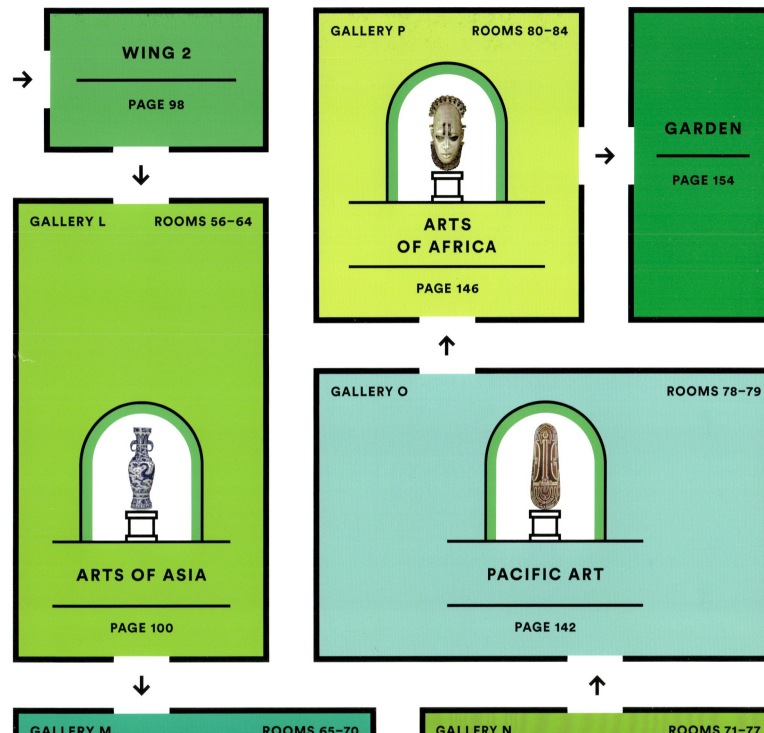
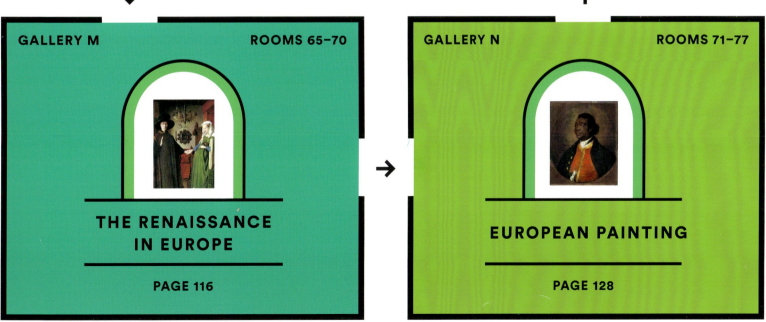

START HERE

Exploring art is like being a detective!

Artworks reveal clues to your own culture and other cultures too. They can show us things that happened before our time, like how people dressed hundreds of years ago or what people ate. They help us think creatively about the times we live in and how different (or similar!) we are to people in the past or even just next door.

This museum is packed full of artworks from all areas of the world. Magnificent pieces that don't usually get to sit side by side can be found together in this museum. Every work of art on display is wonderfully unique, each containing hidden knowledge just waiting to be unlocked.

By exploring the pieces in this museum, you are exploring our world's incredible history of art. Once you've walked through these halls, you'll be well on your way to becoming an art historian.

HELPFUL MUSEUM TIPS

As you move through the museum, you may see the words BCE, CE, and c. as you look at dates. BCE stands for "Before Common Era" and is one clue that something is really ancient. CE stands for "Common Era," which is the time period we live in now. If you see the letter c. before a date, this is short for "circa." It means that the date is the best guess by clever art historians.

There are some fun themes that you can track throughout the galleries too. Simply look out for the eye symbols with interactive questions under some art pieces. These will lead you on a hunt across the book in search of similar themes from different artworks across time and place!

If you get lost, flip to the maps in the gallery introductions. They'll tell you where you are.

You might find words in **bold** that are a mystery. There are clues in the back of the book to help you demystify them!

Finally, if you want a break or a breath of fresh air, don't forget to stop off at the café and garden.

ENJOY YOUR VISIT!

WING

1

IN THE
BEGINNING...

LET'S TRAVEL BACK IN TIME!

Discover treasures from the world's earliest civilizations and the earliest art ever made!

Think of this wing as a time machine that goes back to when people created many things for the first time—the first languages, the first cities and, of course, the first art. Explore how civilizations grew around the world, through the wonderful paintings and objects they created.

INSIDE THIS WING YOU WILL DISCOVER…

- Tombs
- Hidden Treasures
- Heroic Sculptures
- Egyptian Mummies
- Towering Temples
- Mystical Creatures
- Cave Art
- Ancient Empires
- Viking Ships
- Gods and Goddesses
- The Romans
- Greek Myths

GALLERY A
Art of the Stone Age

Begin your museum visit in a gallery filled with ancient artworks. Early carvings and bright paintings show humans living in a very different world. It was a cold and dangerous time, when saber-toothed tigers and mammoths still roamed the earth!

The Stone Age is when early humans first began to make stone tools. It's also when they first created art! We call this time "prehistoric" as it is a period before written history. We can only guess why they made their art, but across the world prehistoric paintings have been found on rocks and hidden deep inside caves.

Stone Age humans were hunters and gatherers who moved around to find food. It was important that the art they made could be carried easily, so sculptures from this time were not as big as the statues and monuments you may see today.

Let's take a look at what kinds of art humans made in the time of stone, ice, and woolly mammoths…

ROOMS 1-2

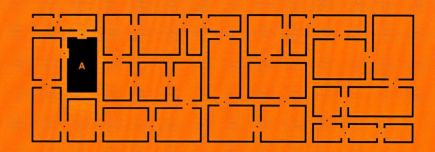

MAP OF THE LAST ICE AGE: AN ANCIENT, ICY WORLD

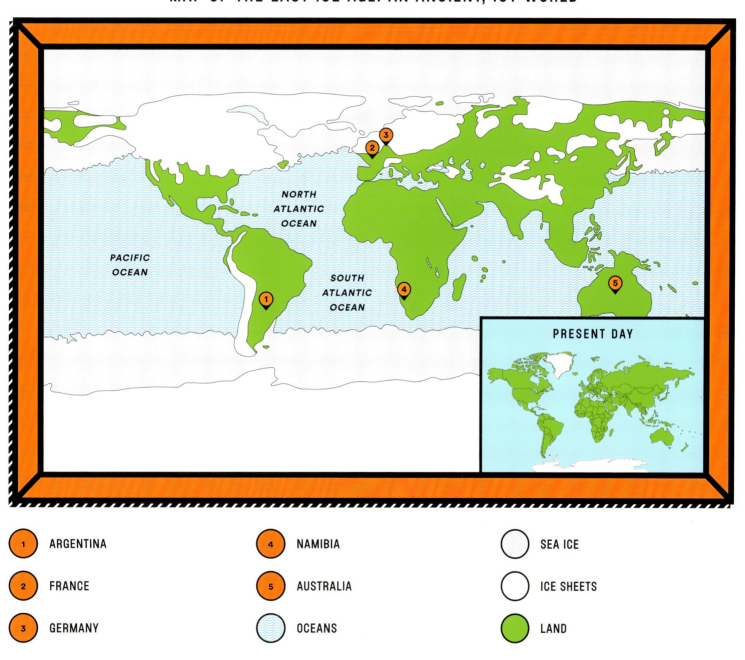

- ① ARGENTINA
- ② FRANCE
- ③ GERMANY
- ④ NAMIBIA
- ⑤ AUSTRALIA
- ○ OCEANS
- ○ SEA ICE
- ○ ICE SHEETS
- ● LAND

Art of the Stone Age 13

ROOM 1

ROCK AND CAVE PAINTINGS
Caves of Wonder

If you don't have paper or canvases to paint on, what do you do? Well, it turns out that cave walls are great places to create artworks, and they last a long time too! Prehistoric humans traveled deep into underground chambers, using simple lamps burning animal fat to

light the way. They created amazing scenes of hunters, animals, and even ritual dances across the cave walls. It's thought that these paintings may be spiritual symbols to make sure that the animals which ancient people needed for food would always be around. Each artwork is a little clue about the past!

WILD ANIMALS

HALL OF THE BULLS, LASCAUX CAVE, c.18,000–15,000 BCE

In 1940, four boys accidentally stumbled across the caves at Lascaux in France while looking for their dog. Little did they know that they had discovered one of the world's greatest sites of prehistoric art. The winding caves include almost 600 prehistoric paintings. In one of the cave's large chambers, named the Hall of Bulls, artists had painted deer, horses, bulls, and other animals. Some of the species, such as giant deer and cave bears, are now extinct. They used **pigments** from plants, stones, and charcoal to put color on the walls.

👁 The animals in this painting were important food sources. If you painted your favorite foods, what would you show?

ROOM 1

SPITTING IMAGES
HAND STENCILS, CUEVA DE LAS MANOS (CAVE OF THE HANDS), c.11,000–7500 BCE

Hands can often be the easiest tools to use for painting. In Argentina's Cueva de las Manos (Cave of the Hands), painters placed their hands on the wall to use as **stencils** and painted around them. They would chew leaves to create a kind of paint, which they could then spit onto walls to leave a colorful handprint.

👁 How many left hands can you count here?

RITUAL DANCE
TASSEL BRADSHAW PAINTING c.19,000 BCE

These rock paintings in Australia show elongated figures wearing special clothing. Can you see the different parts of their outfits, like the frilled sashes around their waist and the arm tassels? Many wear tall hats called headdresses and carry unknown objects that might have been used for ceremonies. In some paintings, the figures seem to run and dance. They may be taking part in a long-lost ritual.

GRAZING ANIMALS
ANCIENT ROCK ART, 1000 BCE–1 CE

This stone shows carvings of cattle with a giraffe extending his long neck over the herd. It is from the site of Twyfelfontein in Namibia, Africa, which is covered with thousands of rock carvings! Stone Age humans lived in this area around 10,000 years ago.

16 The Ultimate Art Museum

OBJECTS OF THE ICE AGE
Art on the Go

ROOM 2

Prehistoric people traveled from place to place as hunter-gatherers. They had not begun to settle down and grow their own food yet. Moving around so much meant they had to carry all their things around with them and sculpt objects into shapes that were small and portable. They carried **figurines**, jewelry, and tools crafted from ivory, bone, and stone. If you had to carry everything with you, which items would you choose?

AS STRONG AS A LION
LION MAN OF HOHLENSTEIN-STADEL, c.31,000 BCE

This part-animal, part-human figure was discovered in Germany. It was originally thought to be a lion man, but some experts now think it depicts a bear man. It is the earliest known zoomorphic (shaped like an animal) **sculpture** discovered on Earth! The maker carved it from a mammoth tusk using stone tools.

HUNTING TOOLS
SCULPTED SPEAR THROWER WEIGHTS, c.15,000–13,000 BCE

Spears were really important for Ice Age humans, who used them to hunt food. They even used carved tools called spearthrowers to help them throw spears farther. Some included weights, like this carved bison, to add speed. This spear weight was discovered in France.

WONDERFUL WOMEN
VENUS OF WILLENDORF, c.25,000 BCE

Venus figurines are little statues of women carved from rock or made of clay. Some people think they are linked to the idea of women becoming mothers. This is the most famous example of around 40 figurines found near Willendorf, Austria. It's only around 4.3 inches tall—that's not even half the size of a Barbie doll. Their small size means they could have been easily carried around.

👁 How does it compare to the figurine on p.36?

Art of the Stone Age 17

GALLERY B
Ancient Near East

Giant sculptures and glistening gold treasures await! Imagine uncovering a lost city filled with the art and riches of people from long ago. Well, this really happened with the discoveries of great, ancient cities buried under earth and sand.

With every corner you turn in the Ancient Near East gallery, you will see stories about the first civilizations on Earth and the large empires they built, starting with Ancient Mesopotamia (modern Iraq) around 3100 BCE. Pretty soon the Mesopotamians were busy inventing the first written language, law codes, and systems for moving food, metals, and other materials across the land and seas. More and more cities grew across the area, which includes the modern countries of Jordan, Syria, Iran, and more.

People developed their own religious beliefs, rituals, and gods, and the art they created tells us about these religions and city life. As people began trading their goods farther and farther away, the empires grew larger, and artists could learn more from each other. Artists in different countries often had similar ideas, such as showing the relationship between humans and the gods. But how they created their art could be very different.

Are you ready to find out more? Let's begin our journey through the first empires.

ROOMS 3–7

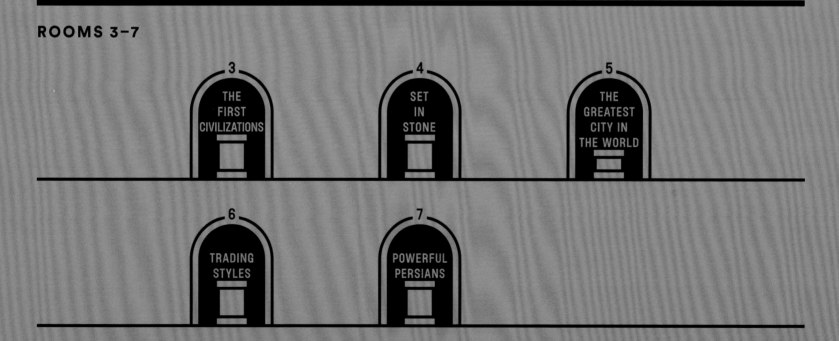

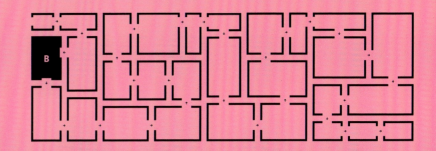

THE GREAT EMPIRES OF THE NEAR EAST

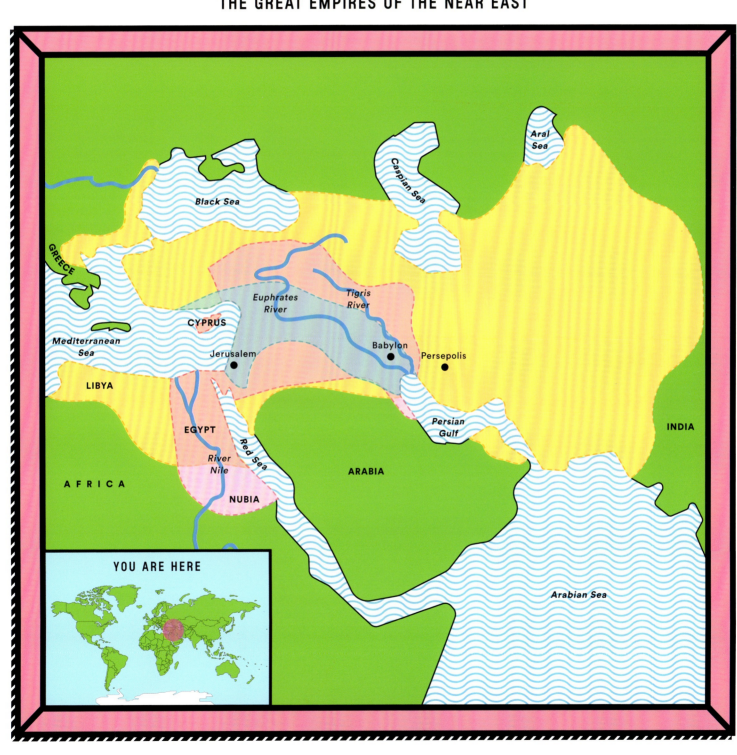

 PERSIAN EMPIRE AT ITS GREATEST   BABYLONIAN EMPIRE AT ITS GREATEST   ASSYRIAN EMPIRE AT ITS GREATEST

Ancient Near East 19

EARLY MESOPOTAMIAN ART
The First Civilizations

ROOM 3

The region of Ancient Mesopotamia (modern-day Iraq) was positioned between the Tigris and Euphrates Rivers. Here there was plenty of water and nutritious soil to grow food and raise animals. The Sumerian civilization and the Akkadian empire, as well as many early cities, flourished here. These Mesopotamian cultures invented the first known writing systems and even the first wheels, which were used to make pottery.

TEMPLE STATUE
SUMERIAN VOTIVE STATUETTE c.2600 BCE

The Sumer civilization was in the south of Mesopotamia. Many **temples** were built to worship gods and goddesses. Statues, like this one, were placed inside these temples to stand in for worshippers when they were not able to be there. The large eyes of this figure would have looked toward a statue of a god.

THE CURSED KING
KING OF AKKAD, c.2250 BCE

Akkad was the world's first great empire. This **Bronze** sculpture is believed to depict the Akkadian king, Naram-Sin, who thought of himself as a god. Ancient **myths** say that the empire became cursed when he stole treasures from the temple of Enlil, the Sumerian god of air and storms. The eye of his statue was later gouged out in protest at his greed.

ROYAL TREASURE
THE STANDARD OF UR, 2600–2400 BCE

In the ancient city of Ur, royal people wanted cemeteries fit for kings and queens. These cemeteries were cut into stone chambers deep below ground. This object was discovered in a tomb, crushed into fragments (4,500 years buried underground can do that!). Now restored, this side shows a scene of war with Sumerian soldiers and wagons. The other side shows a scene of peace.

THE ASSYRIAN EMPIRE
Set in Stone

ROOM 4

After the Akkadians, the Assyrians ruled over northern Mesopotamia (northern Iraq, northeast Syria, and southeastern Turkey) until around 612 BCE. Its cities were filled with impressive buildings and art. Detailed **reliefs**, carved on huge stone slabs, show epic battles, religious scenes, and life in the royal court. These famous Assyrian reliefs were once painted in bright colors and placed in palaces as symbols of royal power.

LIFE IN THE PALACE
KING ASHURNASIRPAL II AND ATTENDANTS, 883–859 BCE

A relief is a kind of sculpture on which the background is carved away, leaving the subject of the work to stand out, like a **three-dimensional** (3D) picture. Many reliefs like this show us how Assyrian royalty lived in this great empire. This larger-than-life relief is over 7 feet tall and was in King Ashurnasirpal II's palace. It shows the king—on the right wearing the crown—surrounded by servants. The details of the clothing and items in the carving help us understand what furniture looked like in the palace and even how people in the royal court dressed, right down to their shoes! The writings and pictures of this relief helped spread the word about the king's great power and success.

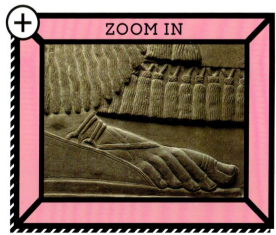

ZOOM IN

Ancient Near East 21

THE BABYLONIAN EMPIRE
The Greatest City in the World

ROOM 5

The Babylonians, who lived in the south of Mesopotamia, fought fiercely and conquered the Assyrian Empire in the north. They built grand palaces and huge cities to show their strength. Many of these buildings were built during the reign of Nebuchadnezzar II (reigned 605–562 BCE). He was one of the most powerful rulers of the time. Eventually, the Assyrian capital of Babylon became the largest city in the world.

MAKING AN ENTRANCE!
ISHTAR GATE, c.605–539 BCE

Upon entering Babylon, visitors were greeted with the massive, brilliant blue Ishtar Gate. This gate made a stunning impression as people entered the inner city. With a height of more than 38 feet, it was about as tall as two giraffes stacked on top of each other! The walls are covered in colorful glazed bricks and have reliefs showing gold dragons, lions, and bulls. These sacred animals were symbols of the gods Marduk, Ishtar, and Adad. The gate is named for Ishtar, the goddess of love and war. Writing on the gate says that King Nebuchadnezzar II wanted to build the gate so that people would look on in wonder, which people are still doing 2,600 years later!

ZOOM IN

EARLY IRANIAN AND THE LEVANTINE ART
Trading Styles

ROOM 6

The ancient Levant region lay to the west of Mesopotamia, and early Iran lay to the east. Across this area people traveled and traded with each other, creating a mix of styles in their art. People of the Levant also traded with neighbors in ancient Greece and Egypt. This explains why Egyptian writing, using hieroglyphs, appears on some of their objects! Sculptures across both regions use stone, metal, ivory, and more.

MYTHICAL BULL
ZEBU VASE, c.1200 BCE

A zebu is a hump-backed bull that appears in a lot of early Iranian art. The nose of this **ceramic** zebu has a spout to pour out liquids. This container and several others like it were found in a cemetery in northern Iran. The zebu could be related to the Persian god Mithras. In mythology, Mithras battled the Bull of Heaven, which held power over the natural world. With Mithras's victory, humans were granted successful harvests by the bull-god.

❓ ART DETECTIVE

Some small objects, such as the zebu vase, were carried across far distances by nomadic cultures. Nomads are people who travel from place to place without a permanent home. This helps them find lush grass to feed their animals.

LOOKING GOOD!
COSMETICS BOX LID, c.1300–1200 BCE

This ivory lid was once part of a makeup box filled with face powder. It shows an ancient nature goddess known as the Mistress of Animals holding out grain to feed two wild goats. Although this piece is from the ancient Near East, her dress and curly hairstyle are similar to popular fashions from ancient Greece. Both men and women in the ancient Near East liked to wear makeup. They crushed colorful gemstones to make a powder then mixed it with water to make eyeshadow and lipstick.

THE PERSIAN EMPIRE
Powerful Persians

ROOM 7

The mighty Babylonian Empire fell at the hands of King Cyrus II of Persia in the year 539 BCE. King Cyrus II and the following kings conquered the lands stretching from Egypt to the Indus River, which became known as the Achaemenid Persian Empire (c.550–330 BCE). It was the world's largest empire at the time! The art celebrated the wealth and power of this new and mighty empire.

A MYTHICAL CHALICE
GRIFFIN RHYTON, c.500–300 BCE

CHARIOT OF FIRE
MODEL CHARIOT, c.500–300 BCE

A rhyton is a container. It has an opening for pouring in liquid and another hole so the liquid can run out. It's used as part of a ritual ceremony. This one is designed as a griffin, a mythical beast that is part eagle, part lion!

The driver of this golden chariot is Bes the Egyptian god of protection, who often appeared in Persian artwork. Both figures are dressed in the style of the Median people of ancient Iran. When their home, in the kingdom of Media, was conquered by King Cyrus II, it became part of the Persian Empire. This object was part of a group of gold and silver treasures discovered near the Oxus River (Amu Darya) in modern Tajikistan.

TRAVELERS FROM AFAR
PERSEPOLIS RELIEFS, c.550–330 BCE

The city of Persepolis was built at the foot of Rahmat Mountain in modern-day southwestern Iraq. As a royal capital of the Achaemenid Empire, it needed grand art and **architecture** to impress visiting officials. Giant sculptures and carvings throughout the capital's buildings showed religious images and people from the empire.

The greatest palace within the city was called the Arpanda, which had a grand audience hall to receive guests. On the pathway leading up to it, relief sculptures showed lines of people bringing gifts to the king. By looking at people's style of clothing and the items they carried, historians have identified a diverse group of people from Egypt, the Nubian kingdom in Africa, Greece, and more. The boots and rounded hats worn by the figures in this relief tell us they may be from an Iranian region called Media.

Ancient Near East 25

GALLERY C
Ancient Egypt

The ancient Egyptians are famous for their giant pyramids, mummies, and secret tombs. But did you know they also loved to invent things? They made the first wigs to protect shaved heads from the sun and even mixed powders to form toothpaste.

Egyptian artists were very important. They were in charge of decorating the insides of tombs and painting the Egyptian ruling royalty—the pharaohs! But artists had to follow strict rules for making their work. When showing ruling royals in paintings or sculptures, they always stood in certain poses and had to be bigger than everyone else.

The people in Egyptian art did not look like real life. The artist usually painted a nose from the side while the eyes would face the front. This was because the ancient Egyptians believed images had power beyond everyday life. They believed showing the full eyes and nose helped paintings to breathe and see. They even painted food on tomb walls to "feed" people in the afterlife!

This is one of the museum's most popular galleries, so try to avoid the crowds as you explore a world of impressive gods and fearless pharaohs.

ROOMS 8–12

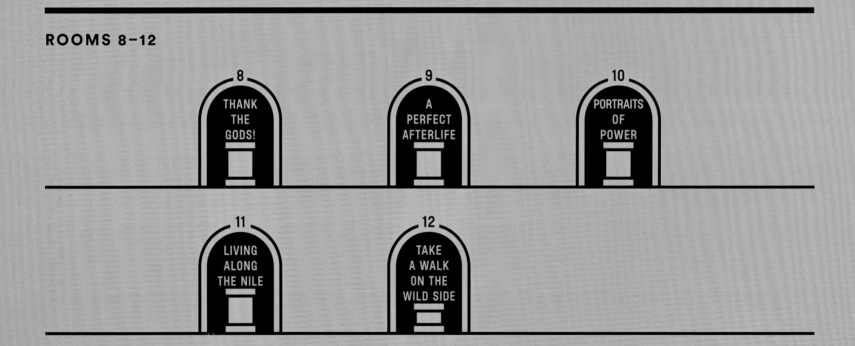

8 THANK THE GODS!
9 A PERFECT AFTERLIFE
10 PORTRAITS OF POWER
11 LIVING ALONG THE NILE
12 TAKE A WALK ON THE WILD SIDE

26 The Ultimate Art Museum

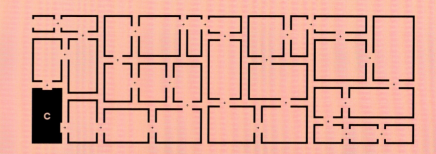

ANCIENT EGYPT: KINGDOMS ALONG THE LUSH RIVER NILE

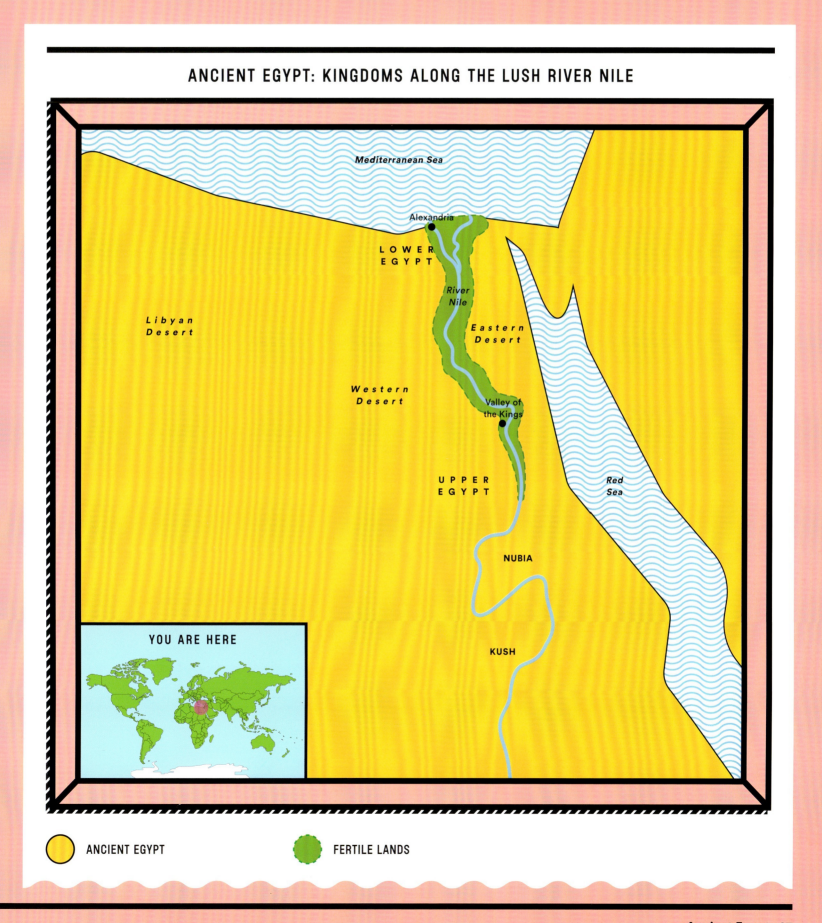

● ANCIENT EGYPT   ● FERTILE LANDS

ROOM 8

EGYPTIAN STATUES
Thank the Gods!

The ancient Egyptians had more than 2,000 gods and goddesses! They believed it was important to recognize and worship them to have a good life, but some were more popular than others. Each god or goddess represented a different part of nature or everyday life. They had special powers and a unique look. They often had the body of a human and the head of an animal, which makes them easy to spot in pictures.

WELL PRESERVED
ANUBIS, 332–30 BCE

FIGHT LIKE A LIONESS
SAKHMET, c.1336–1327 BCE

This statue of Anubis was made of wood and painted plaster. Anubis, the god of death and mummification, is usually shown with a jackal's head on a human body. Mummification is the process of preserving a body after someone dies. All organs except the heart were removed, then the body was covered in salt and left to dry for 40 days. Next, the body was washed, oiled, and wrapped in bandages.

The goddess Sakhmet is shown with the body of a human and the head of a lion. She was a fierce goddess of war and protector of rulers. Even her name meant "powerful one." She was most popular in the ancient Egyptian capital city of Memphis. Sakhmet was also known as the goddess of sickness and healing. Her followers believed she could cure diseases and restore people to good health. The circle above her head is a sun disc.

EGYPTIAN TOMB ART
A Perfect Afterlife

ROOM 9

It may sound grim, but the ancient Egyptians thought a lot about death! Much of the art found from this time was made to give the dead a happy afterlife. Sculptures and paintings in tombs show what people loved and needed. They believed these images would come to life for the person in the next world. The richer a person was, the nicer the tomb. They built the pyramids as the greatest tombs of all for their leaders, the pharaohs!

A FRESH START

NEBAMUN HUNTING IN THE MARSHES, c.1380 BCE

This painting was on a tomb wall belonging to a wealthy man named Nebamun. It shows him hunting wild birds as they fly through the air. The scene is full of fish, cats, birds, and papyrus reeds along the Nile. By hunting the wild animals in the painting, he could have food and a peaceful afterlife with his wife by his side.

? ART DETECTIVE

In ancient Egypt, food was often painted on tomb walls to "feed" people in the afterlife.

Ancient Egypt 29

ROOM 10

ART OF THE PHARAOHS
Portraits of Power

The king of Egypt was called a pharaoh. Pharaohs were usually men, but powerful women such as Hatshepsut (1507–1458 BCE) also ruled with that title. Pharaohs were in charge of government and religion, and were thought of as gods on Earth. Giant sculptures and carvings of pharaohs were put in important spaces, such as temples. You can spot the rulers in pictures by their crown and giant size.

THE CHILD KING
TUTANKHAMUN BURIAL MASK, c.1327 BCE

Tutankhamun was about nine years old when he became a pharaoh. He died ten years later. His tomb was small, but it hid over 5,000 treasures! This mask, made of gold and precious stones, was placed over the head of his mummy to protect it. The cobra on his crown was the symbol of the goddess Wadjet, and could only be worn by a pharaoh.

THE POWERFUL QUEEN
NEFERTITI, c.1352–1336 BCE

This lifelike sculpture shows Queen Nefertiti, whose name means "the Beautiful Woman Has Come." Nefertiti was the chief queen and the most powerful of all of Pharaoh Akhenaten's wives. The sculpture's remaining eye is made of quartz and appears to look out at you! The missing eye was never actually painted.

WINNER TAKES ALL

THUTMOSE III RELIEF, c.1479–1425 BCE

During the first half of his reign, Pharaoh Thutmose III ruled alongside his aunt, Pharoah Hatshepsut. When Hatshepsut died, he led the armies of Egypt to conquer new territories. He built temples and monuments to celebrate his victories. This giant carving of Thutmoss III is a sandstone relief outside of a temple. The outlines are carved into the stone, so the sun can cast strong shadows.

EGYPTIAN CARVINGS
Living Along the Nile

The Nile is the longest river in the world. As a huge water source, it was pretty important in a hot, dry desert. It was full of fish, and very useful for for farming. People in ancient Egypt also bathed and played in the river, making it a busy place. Small carvings show us what daily life was like for people near the Nile. These artworks may look like modern toy models, but they were made thousands of years ago!

COUNT YOUR COWS
INSPECTION OF CATTLE, c.2055–1985 BCE

These models were found in the tomb of an important official named Meketre. In this scene, he is sitting on his porch with four scribes while they take notes about his cattle. In ancient Egypt, cattle were very important. They helped plough fields, and were a source of milk and meat. The more cattle you had, the wealthier you were.

LAND OF THE BOW
NUBIAN ARCHERS, c.2055–1985 BCE

The Nubian region was upstream on the River Nile, to the south of Egypt. The Nubians had their own cultures and kingdoms, like the wealthy kingdom of Kush, which existed for more than 3,000 years. This area is now part of modern Sudan. The Nubians were known for their excellent archery skills. In fact, the Egyptian word for Nubia was *Ta-Seti* and meant "Land of the Bow." This model showing 40 Nubian archers was found in the tomb of an Egyptian governor named Mesheti. A similar group of archers may have defended Mesheti's territory when he was alive.

ANIMAL ART
Take a Walk on the Wild Side

ROOM 12

Pharoahs in Egypt kept dogs, cats, and even cheetahs as pets! There were a lot of wild animals living near their cities, including the crocodiles and hippos that lurked in the River Nile. In Egypt, some animals were thought of as sacred and so they appear again and again in its art. Each animal has a special meaning based on qualities they were known for in real life.

GONE FISHING
FISH VESSEL, c.1330 BCE

Glass bottles like this colorful fish were made to use every day. Historians believe this container was used to hold perfume. The design is shaped like a Nile tilapia fish, which grow and hatch their eggs in the mother fish's mouth!

COOL CATS
GAYER-ANDERSON CAT, c.360 BCE

TROUBLESOME BEASTS
HIPPOPOTAMUS, c.1985–1773 BCE

The Egyptians feared the hippopotamus because it was big and dangerous. But they also believed these animals were a symbol of rebirth (to be born again). This figure was found in a tomb. Three of its legs were purposely broken in ancient times to stop it from causing too much trouble in the afterlife!

This fashionable-looking cat made of bronze shows the goddess Bastet. She was a protector of children. The scarab beetles on her head and chest were symbols of rebirth. Egyptians thought that beetles rolled dung in the same way that Ra, the god of the sun, rolled the sun across the sky to give birth to a new day.

Ancient Egypt 33

GALLERY D
Ancient Greece

The ancient Greeks were great storytellers! They wrote epic stories and dug theaters into the ground to act out dramas. Today, we can see their legendary stories and myths through the art they made.

The ancient Greeks loved art. They made sculptures, pottery, **mosaics**, paintings, and built huge temples from marble and stone. They used their art to pass on myths about gods, heroes, and monsters. They were especially good at making sculptures of people. Using heroes and gods for inspiration, they learnt to sculpt figures that looked incredibly lifelike!

Ancient Greece was not just one country, like modern Greece is today. It was many different city-states. This means each town and city lived by their own rules, even though they shared a common culture, language, and religion.

Throughout the history of art, the ancient Greeks have inspired us with their artistic skill and fantastical storytelling. Even the ancient Romans liked to copy the Greeks. Understanding this era also helps unlock the stories behind centuries of European art.

It's time to find out just what made the Greeks so great!

ROOMS 13–17

13 ISLAND CULTURES
14 EARLY GREEK CIVILIZATIONS
15 THE POTTER'S PLAYGROUND
16 PICTURING THE GODS
17 TRIUMPH OF THE HUMAN FORM

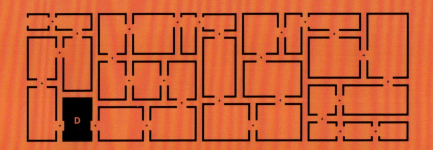

ISLANDS, CULTURES, AND CITIES OF ANCIENT GREECE

ANCIENT GREECE, c.450 BCE

CYCLADIC BRONZE AGE ART
Island Cultures

ROOM 13

The Cyclades are a group of islands forming a circle around the Aegean Sea. *Cyclades* actually means "circle." The home of the ancient Cycladic people was a place full of art. They created the earliest ever examples of landscape paintings and are famous for their marble sculptures. Their streets and buildings were full of bright wall paintings called **frescoes**. These showed plants, animals, and imaginary creatures, like griffins!

PASSING SHIPS
THERA SHIP FRESCO (DETAIL), c.1550 BCE

This fresco shows a group of ships traveling to different ports. Many ancient Greek cities were near coasts or on islands, so sailing by sea was an important way to travel. This is why boats were shown in a lot of their art. At the top left, a herd of deer runs from a lion, as dolphins dance around the ships. This painting is a great example of how people, buildings, and ships looked in ancient times.

CATCH OF THE DAY
FISHERMAN, c.1600–1500 BCE

In this painting, a boy holds two big bundles of dolphinfish. The blue color on his head shows shaved sections, and the two black strips are longer patches of hair. Other Aegean frescos from this time show kids also sporting the same hairstyle to mark the coming of age.

👁 Fishing was an important part of many other cultures and depicted in their art too. Check out p.160.

TRIANGULAR TORSOS
FEMALE FIGURINE, c.2800–2300 BCE

Most Cycladic figurines show women with their arms folded across their body. See how the **form** is made with a triangular head and body? This is what we call an **abstract** style of art because it does not look realistic. Later, you can spot artists in wing three who were inspired by these designs.

👁 Do you see another object with triangular, abstract figures on p.38?

MINOAN AND MYCENAEAN ART
Early Greek Civilizations

ROOM 14

The Minoan civilization was based on the island of Crete and was named after the mythical King Minos. The Minoans were leaders in building and making art. The Mycenaean civilization arose on mainland Greece and later conquered the Minoans. The Mycenaeans spoke an early form of Greek. Both cultures existed during the Bronze Age and made many important objects of gold and silver, as well as bronze.

DO NOT BREAK!
WISHBONE-HANDLED CUP c.1400 BCE

The handle of this bowl is one wishbone you wouldn't want to break! The shape of the cup was popular in Cyprus, where it was found. The gold bull and flower decorations—made with a technique called inlay—are in a Mycenaean style.

GOLDEN CHALICE
VAPHEIO CUPS, c.1475 BCE

This is one of a pair of golden cups found in a tomb near Sparta. The designs show hunters trying to capture a wild bull, with a rope round his leg. The tomb belonged to a wealthy Mycenaean, but the cups seem to have been made in the Minoan style.

DECORATIVE BLADES
INLAID DAGGER, c.1550–1500 BCE

Just like the wishbone-handled cup above, the design on this dagger was made with inlaid silver and gold. Two lions run away on the right while one attacks a man on the ground. To the left, hunters use their shields and spears to capture the beast. The technique of making pictures with metal is thought to have come from Syria. Daggers like these are linked to the skilled craftwork from the island of Crete.

Ancient Greece 37

ROOM 15

GREEK POTTERY
The Potter's Playground

The ancient Greeks are famous for their pottery. You can find clues about how their pottery was used by looking at the shape. Storage vases had smaller necks while vases for mixing were large with a bigger opening. They were also painted with scenes from everyday life or from dramatic stories. As pottery can last a long time, it is useful for archaeologists looking to learn how people lived in ancient Greece.

PATTERNS IN CLAY

HIRSCHFELD KRATER, c.750 BCE

The Geometric Period (c.900–700 BCE) was a time when painters used simple patterns and shapes on pottery. Vases like this one did not hold anything, but were used to mark the graves in a cemetery of ancient Athens. The images show people in mourning, and some are even tearing their hair out in grief!

👁 Vases come in all shapes and sizes! See p.111.

SEEING RED

EUPHRONIOS AND EUXITHEOS DEATH OF SARPEDON, c.515 BCE

This is called red-figure pottery because the background is black with figures appearing red because of the color of Athens' clay. It shows Sarpedon, a son of Zeus. When he died, Zeus asked the gods of sleep and death to bring him home.

A TALE OF TWO HEADS

JANIFORM ARYBALLOS, 510 BCE

One half of this vase shows the head of an Ethiopian person in black and the other half shows a Greek woman in the red clay. The writing on the side says *kalos*, which means "beautiful."

38   The Ultimate Art Museum

MYTHICAL ART
Picturing the Gods

ROOM 16

Have you ever wondered why the seasons change or what makes flowers bloom in spring? Today, science can give us the reasons. In ancient Greece, myths were used to explain why things happen in nature. These were the stories of gods, humans, and heroes. Greek myths were not written down until much later, so mosaics, paintings, and sculpture were one colorful way they told these stories instead.

EXPLAINING THE SEASONS

HADES AND PERSEPHONE, c.340 BCE

This painting shows Hades, the god of the underword, with Persephone as they ride a chariot together. Persephone lived part of the year with Hades and part of it on Earth. When Persephone was away in the underworld during the winter, her mother, the goddess of grain, was sad. She didn't allow plants to grow until spring, when Persephone reappeared. This was how the Greeks explained the change in seasons. This painting is on the back of a marble throne, found in a tomb for Queen Eurydice I of Macedon.

HAVE COURAGE!

DIONYSOS ON A LEOPARD, c.330–300 BCE

Dionysos was the god of festivity and grape harvests. He is often shown riding a leopard or wearing its skin. Pictures of hunting or wild animals, like this one, were symbols of strength and courage. This floor **mosaic** is made from thousands of small pebbles, terracotta (clay that is fired), and lead, set in cement.

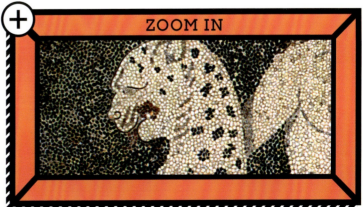

ZOOM IN

Ancient Greece 39

GREEK SCULPTURES
Triumph of the Human Form

Over hundreds of years, Greek artists became masters at creating sculptures of the human body. At first, figures looked stiff and did not have much detail (see *Kroisos*). During the Hellenistic period (323–27 BCE), artists were much better at showing realistic muscles and emotions. While it might look like ancient Greece was full of white sculptures, they were originally painted in bright colors.

REST IN PEACE
KROISOS, *c.*530 BCE

A kouros is a nude sculpture of a young man. Sculptures of young women, always clothed, are called kore. This example was a grave marker for Kroisos, a soldier who died in battle. Greek sculptures like this were inspired by Egyptian sculptures. The Greeks gave their early statues more life by separating the arms from the body.

BURIED TREASURE
RIACE WARRIORS, *c.*460–440 BCE

This is one of two famous bronze warrior sculptures discovered by divers off the coast of Italy. One of the figure's legs is relaxed, with most of his weight on the other foot. This curved pose is called contrapposto. It was a new way of showing people in less stiff and more natural poses. The warrior would have originally worn a helment and carried a shield and spear.

SPREAD YOUR WINGS
NIKE OF SAMOTHRACE, *c.*180 BCE

Nike was the goddess of victory—you can often recognize her by her wings. This sculpture, made of marble, was set in a fountain. Her dress looks heavy and clings close to the shape of her body. This style is called wet-drapery because her clothes look soaking wet. This is one of the most celebrated sculptures in the world. Many copies exist, and a World Cup trophy was based on it!

A LABOR OF LOVE

HAGESANDROS OF ANTIOCH ON THE MAEANDER, VENUS DE MILO, LATE 100s BCE

LIKE FATHER LIKE SON

HAGESANDROS, ATHENEDOROS, AND POLYDOROS OF RHODES (ATTRIB.), LAOCOÖN, COPY AFTER 300–100 BCE ORIGINAL

Over the centuries, this marble sculpture has lost its jewelry, headband, and even its arms! Art historians think she is either Aphrodite, the goddess of love, or the sea goddess Amphitrite. Her missing arms and anything she was holding may have given the clue to her true identity. Gods often held something that told us who they were. For example, Poseidon, god of the sea, always held a trident.

This Roman copy of a Greek sculpture shows the Trojan priest Laocoön and his two sons. Laocoön tried to convince the Trojans not to accept a gift from the Greeks— the famous Trojan horse—because he knew it was a trick! The goddess Athena (protector of the cunning Greeks) became angry and sent serpents to attack Laocoön. He is seen here writhing in pain.

? ART DETECTIVE

This sculpture was lost for over 1,000 years! When it was rediscovered, it was a huge inspiration to Michelangelo (see p.121).

Ancient Greece 41

GALLERY E
Etruscans and Ancient Romans

The ancient Romans were among the most powerful conquerors in ancient history. Their empire stretched across parts of Africa, Europe, and Asia too!

Before the Roman Republic was founded in Italy, around 509 BCE, there were a group of people called the Etruscans. They lived in Etruria, the central region of what is now Italy. Much of what we know about the Etruscans comes from their unique art and what other civilizations wrote about them. Since none of their own writing is still around, they're often called "mysterious." Fortunately, much of their art and culture was absorbed by the Romans, who ruled the area after them.

The art of the Roman Republic and then the Roman Empire was inspired by the different cultures across Africa, Asia, southern Europe, and especially the Greeks. Roman art includes colossal architecture, great sculptures, mosaics, paintings, and more! Their clever recipe for concrete even allowed them to build huge buildings, such as Rome's Colosseum, which is still around today.

In the course of their long history, the Romans created a style that would inspire European artists for years to come. Let's delve into the world of Etruscans and ancient Roman art!

ROOMS 18–23

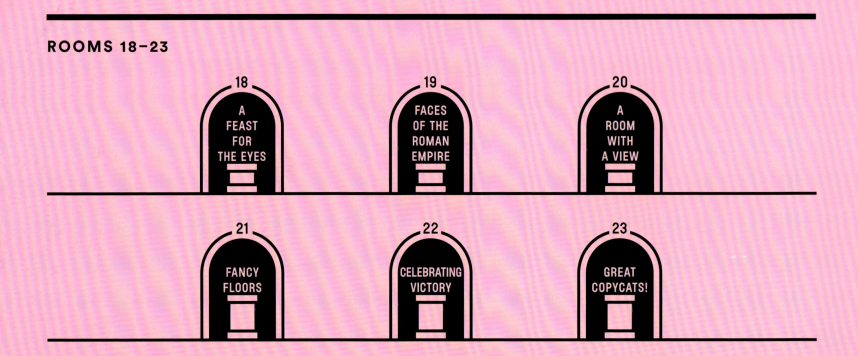

18 A FEAST FOR THE EYES
19 FACES OF THE ROMAN EMPIRE
20 A ROOM WITH A VIEW
21 FANCY FLOORS
22 CELEBRATING VICTORY
23 GREAT COPYCATS!

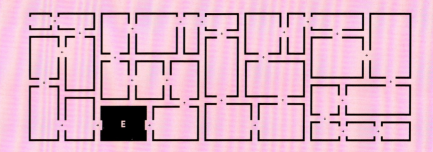

THE MIGHTY ROMAN EMPIRE

ROMAN EMPIRE AT ITS GREATEST, 117 CE

Etruscans and Ancient Romans 43

ROOM 18

ETRUSCAN ART
A Feast for the Eyes

The Etruscans were once a powerful Mediterranean civilization. They were skilled at working with bronze, terracotta, stone, and gold. Their art includes tomb paintings and bronze sculptures made to celebrate the afterlife. The color and drama in their paintings were often inspired by the Greeks. That's why these artworks are a helpful way to see how some lost Greek wall paintings may have looked.

WILD CAT GUARDIANS
TOMB OF THE LEOPARDS, c.475 BCE

Funerals were a big deal to the Etruscans! This wall painting was made for a rock-cut tomb in a large ancient cemetery in Tarquinia, Italy. This cemetery contains 6,000 graves and 200 tombs decorated with frescos. This tomb shows the funeral celebrations of a deceased person, including dancers, musicians, and a big banquet. Look closely and you can see a man offering a woman an egg. The egg is a symbol of life after death. Further along the scene, above the banquet, two large leopards watch over, giving the tomb its name.

44 The Ultimate Art Museum

ROMAN SCULPTURES
Faces of the Roman Empire

ROOM 19

If you were to become the new ruler of a huge empire, how would you let everyone know? The Romans used big sculptures. Artists in Rome carved portraits of the emperor's head (called **busts**) and sent them around the empire for others to copy in paintings and sculptures. Portraits of the emperor appeared in many public places, like markets, plazas, and parks, so everyone would know who ruled and what they looked like.

THE FIRST EMPEROR OF ROME
AUGUSTUS OF PRIMA PORTA, c.20 BCE

Augustus Caesar (63 BCE–14 CE) was the first Roman emperor. Here, Augustus is dressed like a great military leader. At the bottom of this 6-foot-tall marble statue, baby Cupid is riding a dolphin. This is because the emperor's family said they were descended from Cupid's mother, the goddess Venus. Sculptures like these were originally painted in shockingly bright colors!

EMPEROR AS A GOD
CLAUDIUS, c.42–43 BCE

Emperor Claudius (10 BCE–54 CE) was the fourth Roman emperor. He was famous for his great accomplishments, such as extending the Roman Empire into North Africa and the faraway island of Britain. This massive marble sculpture shows Claudius as Jupiter, king of the Roman gods and the god of thunder. The eagle at the bottom is a clue because the eagle is Jupiter's bird.

Etruscans and Ancient Romans

ROOM 20

WALL PAINTINGS
A Room with a View

We are usually taught not to draw or paint on the walls, but that's exactly what the Romans did! Bright frescos, or wall paintings, were popular decorations inside homes. Some frescos featured painted columns or scenes from the countryside. Others showed dramatic tales about gods or heroes. Paint was applied while the plaster was still wet—the paintings then dried as part of the wall and could last hundreds of years.

NATURE'S BEAUTY

CUBICULUM, VILLA OF PUBLIUS FANNIUS SYNISTOR, 40–30 BCE

When the volcano Mount Vesuvius erupted in 79 CE, it buried the nearby city of Pompeii in ash. The ash and rock completely covered the art and architecture of the buildings and ended up protecting them. When they were uncovered hundreds of years later, excellent examples of art were discovered intact! These can show us how the Romans once lived. Take a look at this bedroom, for example. It was once part of a villa, a mile away from the destroyed city of Pompeii. Once the dirt was cleaned away, the wall paintings showed beautiful outdoor architecture and rocky landscapes. These frescos could remind their owners of the brilliant landscapes outside.

46 The Ultimate Art Museum

MOSAICS

Fancy Floors

ROOM 21

Picture yourself walking into a building. Where would you look to find works of art? In ancient Rome, you might try looking down. Many Roman buildings were decorated with detailed pictures on the floor made from thousands of tiny tiles. These are called mosaics. Artists used lots of different tiles so that images could have as much detail as a painting.

AFTER THE FEAST
HERAKLEITOS UNSWEPT ROOM, EARLY 200s CE

This mosaic shows what a messy floor might have looked like after a big feast! Berries, bones, shells, and even birds' feet were part of this design for a dining-room floor. See how lifelike some of it looks? The artist even added tiled shadows on each piece, as if light is hitting it from above—what a thoughtful detail!

? ART DETECTIVE

Some houses had the mosaic inscription: "Cave Canem." This is Latin for "Beware of the Dog"!

Etruscans and Ancient Romans 47

ROOM 22

COLUMNS
Celebrating Victory

Many people like to celebrate when they achieve something. Today we might throw a party, but the ancient Romans preferred something more permanent. After winning a hard battle or war, they sometimes put up a tall column as a symbol of the victory. These could be seen far and wide. Victory columns usually had a statue of the ruler on top and some, like Trajan's Column, had reliefs carved onto the sides.

INTO BATTLE!

PROFECTIO SCENE, TRAJAN'S COLUMN 113 CE

To celebrate conquering Dacia (modern Romania), Emperor Trajan (reigned 98–117 CE) had this huge column made. It was placed in a new public space in Rome called Trajan's Forum. The pictures on the side show the Roman army building forts, gathering supplies and charging into battle. A sculpture of Trajan (naturally!) was at the top, but it was later removed. The column is almost 98 feet high and made of twenty hollow marble pieces. A spiral staircase of marble inside the column meant that visitors could climb up to a platform at the top. When Trajan died, his ashes were kept in a compartment at the base of the column. The reliefs can be looked at like a comic strip. The viewer can see a story that spirals from bottom to top.

👁 Who else celebrates victory with a relief sculpture? See p.31.

ROMAN SCULPTURE
Great Copycats!

ROOM 23

If you want to know more about Greek sculpture, the best place to look is ancient Rome! The Romans were great admirers (and copiers) of the Greeks. They also adopted the Greek gods, such as Aphrodite, who the Romans called Venus. They decorated their homes and public spaces with Greek-inspired sculpture. Statues could be made of gods and heroes or important villagers and relatives.

WATCHFUL FACES

MAN CARRYING PORTRAIT HEADS, EARLY 100s CE

This marble sculpture shows a man standing with the **busts** of two of his ancestors. Romans sometimes carried wax or plaster busts of the dead during funeral processions. Rich Romans would then keep their ancestors' busts in their homes. Young people would have thought twice about being naughty under the watchful eye of their elders!

AN EARLY BATH

CAPITOLINE VENUS, c.200s CE

Here the goddess Venus stands next to a vase used for bathing. The fabric draped over the vase is a clue that this is a Roman copy of a Greek sculpture. Can you see how the figure is leaning against it? Roman copies made of marble need more support than the original bronze statues made by the Greeks.

Etruscans and Ancient Romans 49

GALLERY F
The Byzantine World

Historians call this group of people the Byzantines, but they thought of themselves as Romans. Why? Because the Roman empire had split in two and the Byzantines lived in the eastern half. This was a time with many changes, including new art styles!

After Constantine the Great became the emperor of the Roman Empire, he moved its capital from Rome to Byzantium (modern Istanbul) in the year 330 CE. This is where the Byzantine name comes from, though he renamed the city Constantinople. Constantine was the first Roman emperor to convert to Christianity, a religion that believes in Jesus as the son of God. From Constantine onward, almost all Roman emperors were Christian. Many ordinary followers of ancient religions also converted to Christianity.

With the change to Christianity, the art in this time changed too. Large churches were built and decorated with elaborate religious art. As you explore the halls of this gallery, you'll see how artists made new art styles for books, paintings, sculptures, and mosaics. Even after the Empire was gone, artists across Europe continued to make works inspired by the decorative Byzantine style. Shall we have a look?

ROOMS 24–27

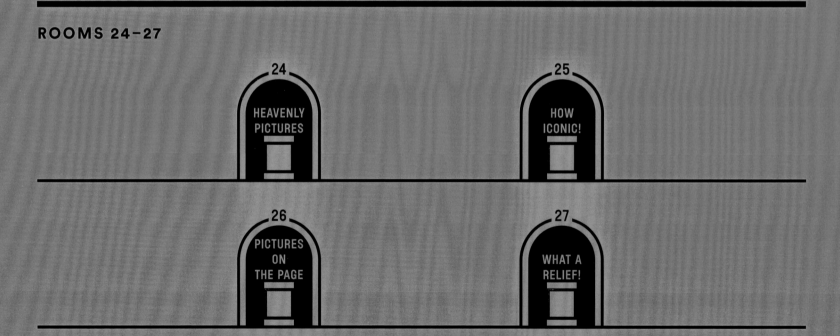

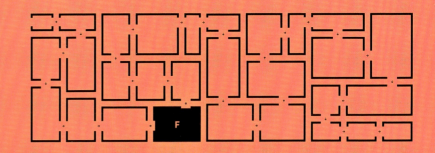

The Byzantine World: Strength of the Eastern Roman Empire

- - - - BYZANTINE EMPIRE AT ITS GREATEST

BYZANTINE MOSAICS
Heavenly Pictures

ROOM 24

Inside the first big Christian churches there were colorful mosaics. These looked similar to ancient Roman mosaics, but Byzantine artists were interested in creating scenes that looked like heavenly pictures. One way they did this was by showing figures on glittering gold backgrounds. Pictures of saints helped people feel connected to the spiritual world, and images of rulers showed that they supported the church, too.

WHO'S THE BOSS?

EMPEROR JUSTINIAN AND HIS COURT, 547–549 CE

Justinian I, also called Justinian the Great, supported the building of many new structures, which allowed art and architecture to flourish during his reign. This mosaic from the church of San Vitale in Ravenna, Italy, shows Justinian at the center of a group of important administrators and church officials. The image is full of **symbolism** if you know where to look! Justinian wears a crown and purple robe—both symbols of royalty—and is holding bread for the Christian ritual of communion. To the far left, a soldier holds a shield with an overlapping P and X design that represents Christ and Christianity.

ICONS
How Iconic!

ROOM 25

Byzantine art has many images of Christ and other Christian figures. We call these "icons." Artists made these glittering, colorful images to go inside churches, some public buildings, and homes. Christians would pray in front of these icons, which were seen as holy objects. For a time in the 800s CE, people worried that God would be angry at them for worshipping artworks, and many of them were destroyed.

HEAVENLY PROTECTOR
ICON OF THE ARCHANGEL MICHAEL, 1100s CE

This gold and enamel icon shows the Archangel Michael guarding the gates of heaven with a sword. The edges are decorated with smaller pictures of saints and precious stones, and an image of Christ is just above Michael's head. Layers of enamel were built up to create three-dimensional areas, like the angel's wings and legs.

THE ALL-POWERFUL ONE
CHRIST PANTOKRATOR, 500s CE

Christ Pantokrator images, like this one, show a specific style of Christ in pictures. He is usually shown with a book, a circular halo around his head and his right hand raised in blessing. Pantokrator means "all-powerful," and this is the earliest example of this style and one of the oldest surviving Byzantine icons.

The Byzantine World

ROOM 26

ILLUMINATED MANUSCRIPTS

Pictures on the Page

An illuminated manuscript is like a picture book, filled with colorful illustrations! A book is "illuminated" if the pages are decorated with hand-drawn pictures or elaborate letters. Each one is one-of-a-kind because they're done completely by hand. Artists working in monasteries wrote about history and religion, then decorated these texts with patterns, pictures, and even gold.

GREAT SERMONS!

SCENES FROM THE OLD TESTAMENT, PARIS GREGORY, c.879–83 CE

These are illustrations from a book known as the Paris Gregory, which is filled with sermons of Saint Gregory the Great. This page shows three scenes from the Old Testament, which is the first half of the Christian Bible. The top image shows Abraham, who is about to sacrifice his son Isaac before being stopped by an angel. The middle shows Isaac's son Jacob having a vision while dreaming. The bottom scene shows the prophet Samuel as he blesses David, the King of Israel—the same David who defeats the giant Goliath. Because these books took so long to make and were so beautifully decorated, people took care of them over time—even if they couldn't read. These books were so precious that some emperors held them during important ceremonies.

? ART DETECTIVE

Making these books was hard work! The pages, made from animal skin called vellum, was cut and poked with guidelines so that the text ran straight. Artists added decorations before the pages were sewn together into a book.

54 The Ultimate Art Museum

RELIEF SCULPTURES
What a Relief!

ROOM 27

The Byzantines liked to make relief sculptures and small objects from elephant tusks. This material is called ivory and, unfortunately for elephants, it was used a lot. Tusks could be cut lengthways to make panels or cut across to make small sculptures and boxes. The Byzantines preferred to carve panel reliefs instead of sculptures. The reliefs were often painted in bright colors, which made them pop out!

A SPECIAL ANNOUNCEMENT
IVORY WITH THE ANNUNCIATION, LATE 700s CE OR EARLY 800s CE

This panel shows the angel Gabriel visiting the Virgin Mary to tell her she will become a mother to Jesus, the son of God. The columns and doorways in the background are carved with different depths and textures. This gives the appearance of a big room on the small, flat surface.

THE GREAT CHASE
DIPTYCH LEAF WITH A HUNT SCENE, EARLY 500s CE

The top of this panel shows three men seated in an arena watching a stag hunt. Down below, hunters are shown chasing animals to entertain a crowd. This is one of two panels that belonged together. Two paintings or panels that are part of the same artwork are called a **diptych**.

The Byzantine World 55

GALLERY G
The Islamic World

Math, religion, and art join forces in this gallery! Early art from the Islamic world can be found in North Africa, Spain, and India, as well as throughout Middle Eastern countries. The art made across these areas includes colorful mosaics, bold geometric patterns, and mighty architecture.

The Islamic religion spread through trade networks and growing empires. This gallery will highlight just some of the shared themes found throughout the early Islamic world. Some of the art in this gallery is religious, but not all of it. Some of the makers were Muslim (followers of the religion Islam), but not all of them. The word *Islam* comes from the Arabic word for "peace," and the Muslim name for God is Allah.

Islam began with the Prophet Muhammad in Makkah (modern Mecca, Saudi Arabia) around 610 CE. Allah spoke to Muhammad through the angel Jibril, and Muhammad wrote down what he heard. This writing became the holy book, the Qur'an. In the rooms to come, you'll discover how artists have used decorative patterns and writing from the Qur'an to make stunning art.

ROOMS 28–30

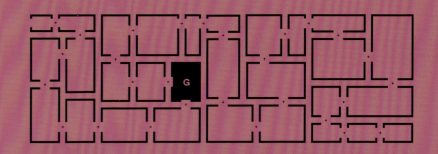

EARLY ISLAMIC WORLD: THE FIRST DYNASTIES

● THE ISLAMIC WORLD, 750 CE

THE FIRST DYNASTY
Building a Kingdom

ROOM 28

A dynasty is a family, or group, that rules for a period of time. The first dynasty in the Islamic world began in 661 CE with the Umayyads. In less than ten years, the Umayyads grew their empire to be the biggest in the world! They created important works of early Islamic art, including desert palaces with impressive mosaics. These palaces are still standing and are just as splendid as they were 1,000 years ago.

THE BALANCE OF POWER
AUDIENCE ROOM MOSAIC, c.740 CE

An audience room is where rulers would see guests or have ceremonies. This floor mosaic was found in an Umayyad desert palace in Palestine. It shows three gazelles and a lion.

MOSQUE ARCHITECTURE
Art and Prayer

ROOM 29

Muslims pray, learn, and meet with each other at the mosque. Mosque buildings can be truly impressive, elaborately decorated, and include different sections with special purposes. Tall towers called *minarets* are where the call to prayer is announced five times a day. When Muslims pray, they face Mecca, where the Prophet Muhammad was born. A niche in the wall, called a *mihrab*, shows you where to face.

COLORFUL COMPASS
MIHRAB, GREAT MOSQUE OF CORDOBA, 961–976 CE

This tiled *mihrab* is found in the Great Mosque of Cordoba, Spain, a city that was once the capital of the Umayyad dynasty. A year after becoming the caliph (ruler), Al-Hakam II had this new, massive *mihrab* built in the mosque. All the other *mihrabs* in the mosque are small nooks, but this one is the size of an entire room.

LESSONS IN LIGHT
MOSQUE WINDOW, 1125

This window is part of the Al-Aqmar (moonlit) mosque in Cairo. The window design has a hanging lamp (representing Earth) and a star (for the heavens). It could be a visual way of understanding a verse in the Qur'an that describes God as "the light of the heavens and the earth."

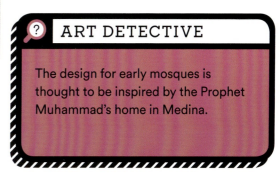

ART DETECTIVE

The design for early mosques is thought to be inspired by the Prophet Muhammad's home in Medina.

The Islamic World 59

ROOM 30

DESIGNS FROM THE ISLAMIC WORLD
Patterns and Writing

Islamic artists used elaborate patterns and writing to decorate buildings and objects. Common styles include overlapping floral designs and **geometric** patterns made of different shapes. Islamic religious art sometimes used calligraphy (decorative writing) to create interesting designs. The two main writing styles are Kufic (the oldest, with thick, straight lines) and the curvier Naskh style displayed here.

MIGHTY METAL
MOHAMMAD IBN AL-ZAYN, BAPTISTERY OF ST LOUIS, c.1320–1340

This brass basin is packed with action! The images were hammered on. You'll find riders hunting bears, a unicorn chasing an elephant, a figure slaying a dragon, and more. The original purpose of this vessel is unknown, but it was later used to baptize French royal children for hundreds of years. It was originally made by Muhammad ibn al-Zayn, a craftsman from the Mamluk dynasty in modern Syria and Egypt.

For another knight slaying a dragon, go to p.118.

ZOOM IN

FIT FOR A SULTAN

ALI IBN MUHAMMAD AL-ASHRAFI AND IBRAHIM AL-AMIDI, QUR'AN OPENING PAGES, 1372

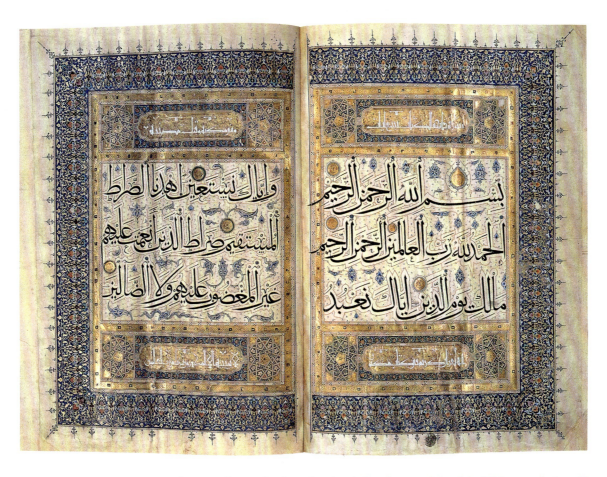

This Qur'an was made for a sultan (a Muslim ruler) named Barsbay. Colorful designs around the sides of these pages combine patterns commonly found in the Islamic world with Chinese lotus flower designs. It shows how trade with faraway places, such as China, inspired artists to try new styles.

LIGHT FOR THE DEAD

MOSQUE LAMP, c.1285

Glass lamps were filled with oil and hung from the ceiling to give off light. The writing tells us this lamp was for the tomb of Aydakin ibn 'abd Allah. During his life, he was a bow-keeper to the ruler, so two golden crossbows are shown over a red shield.

ZOOM IN

The Islamic World 61

GALLERY H
Medieval Europe

Some people call early medieval times the Dark Ages, but don't believe what they tell you! A dark age does not usually have many inventions, written records, or art. But as you will discover in this gallery, there was a lot of all these things.

The medieval period in Europe lasted from around the 400s to the 1200s. This was a period of change and of invasions. Tribes, such as the Vandals, Anglo-Saxons, and Goths, migrated all over Europe. The Huns invaded from Central Asia and then, later, the Vikings sailed out from the frosty north to do their share of invading. All of this can be seen through the art on display.

It was only after the year 800 CE, during the reign of Charlemagne (Charles the Great), that life in western and central Europe began to settle down. Charlemagne became emperor of the Holy Roman Empire, which stretched across much of Europe. At this time, more and more people converted to Christianity. Monks painted religious texts and perfected book writing, and huge cathedrals were built with impressive sculptures. The colorful Romanesque style emerged around the year 950 CE and the dramatic Gothic style around 1150.

It's time to open the door to some amazing art from medieval Europe.

ROOMS 31–36

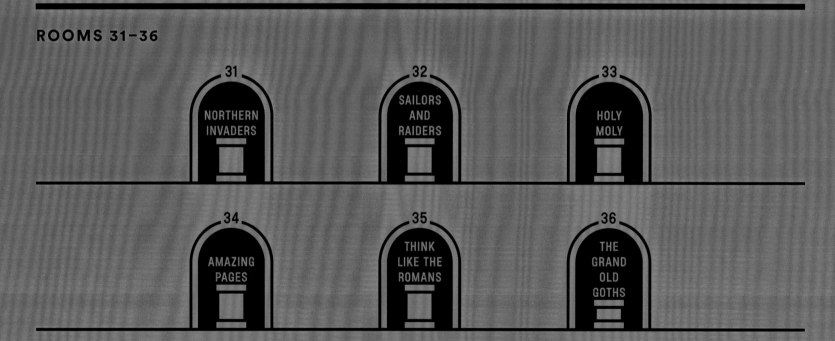

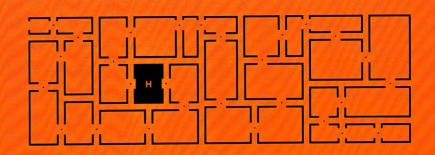

MEDIEVAL EUROPE: CHANGING NATIONS

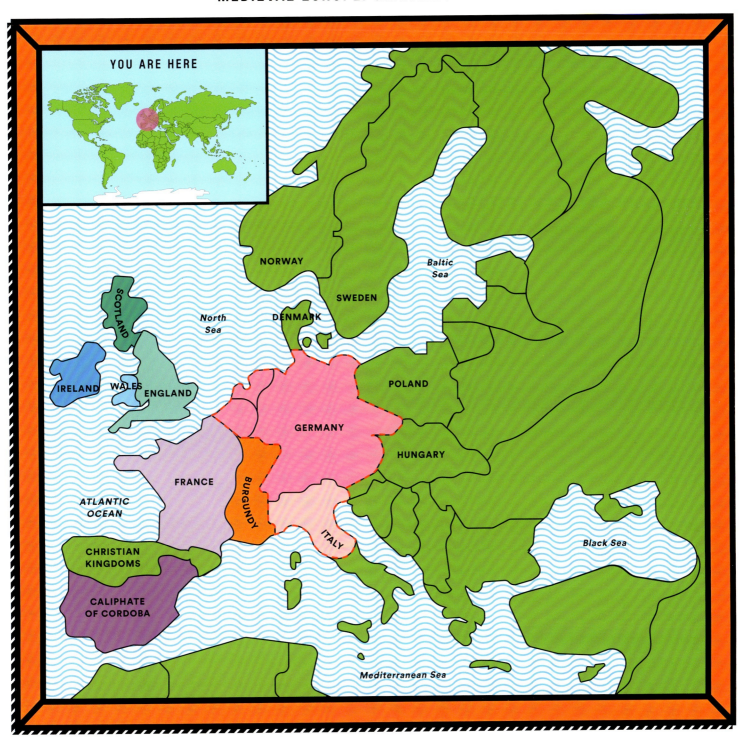

- - - - HOLY ROMAN EMPIRE

ROOM 31

ANGLO-SAXON ENGLAND
Northern Invaders

The Angles and Saxons were people who traveled from present-day Germany to live in Britain around the 400s CE. We now call this group the Anglo-Saxons. Some of the most amazing examples of their art came from an entire ship that was buried underground at Sutton Hoo in England. The ship was a tomb for an important person, possibly King Redwald of East Anglia, who died around 624 CE.

HERE BE DRAGONS!

PARADE HELMET, c.600–650 CE

Although this metal helmet was buried in a grave for more than 1,300 years, you can still see the detailed face design. The eyebrows, nose, and moustache come together to form a flying dragon. You can also make out the gold tips shaped like a boar's head bursting from the ends of its wings.

> **ART DETECTIVE**
>
> The wood from the buried ship at Sutton Hoo rotted away centuries ago, leaving only a ship-shaped hole filled with treasure!

BLINGIN' BELTS

GOLD BUCKLE, c.580–620 CE

The Anglo-Saxons needed a way to keep their trousers up, just like the rest of us! This stunning golden belt buckle is covered in interlacing shapes of snakes, birds, and hidden animals. Many of the treasures inside the Sutton Hoo site show the way that the Anglo-Saxons loved objects made with expensive materials.

VIKINGS
Sailors and Raiders

ROOM 32

The Vikings were known for being excellent sailors. They lived in Scandinavia (present-day Denmark, Norway, and Sweden) but traveled to other lands and raided villages. Much of the Viking art that exists was made from long-lasting materials, such as stone and metal. The art was filled with designs of knotted patterns or images of animals, such as serpents, horses, and fantastical beasts.

WOMEN OF POWER
STORA HAMMARS STONE, c.750 CE

The Stora Hammars Stone from Sweden is an excellent example of **narrative art**. This is one of four stones that was placed outside and shows stories from ancient Scandinavian mythology. Here we see a Viking longship, a Valkyrie, and a sacrifice. Valkyries were powerful, mythical women who decided who lived and who died in battle. Hildr, the Valkryie in this scene, could bring warriors back to life.

SHIVER ME TIMBERS
HEGGEN VANE, c.1000s

If you go sailing, you may want a weather vane, like this one, to show you which way the wind is blowing. The Vikings had many useful objects like this on their ships. This one is covered in plants and a dragon, which was a popular beast among the Vikings. The design is called the Ringerike style, named after an area in Norway. Holes on the edges once held streamers or pendants that chimed and moved in the wind.

+ **ZOOM IN**

Medieval Europe

CHRISTIAN SHRINES
Holy Moly

ROOM 33

When an object is very special, it's a good idea to keep it in a safe place. During the medieval period, the Christian church started keeping the possessions and even body parts of important people, such as saints and popes, in containers called reliquaries or shrines. People believed these remains, called **relics**, had spiritual powers. Sometimes, the shape of the reliquary referred to what it held inside.

STAND FOR YOUR BELIEFS!
RELIQUARY OF SAINT FAITH, c.950 CE

Saint Faith was a young Christian girl who refused to offer gifts to Roman gods, no matter what! To Christians, the Roman gods were not to be worshipped. The saint's skull can be found in this reliquary's head. The head was made from an old Roman parade helmet from the 400s CE. Visitors to the reliquary in France donated gems and gold, which were added over time. It was given a crown in the late 900s CE, and its new feet were added in the 1800s.

GOLDEN TOUCH
SHRINE OF ST ANDREW'S SANDAL, 977–993 CE

Can you guess what is in this box, topped with a golden foot? This shrine in Germany is said to hold part of a sandal worn by Saint Andrew, a follower of Christ. It was made to be easily carried around by bishops and kings, so it's only 17.3 inches long. A relic like this was believed to hold power, especially if it had come into contact with a saint. Some relics were even carried into battle for luck.

BOOK OF KELLS
Amazing Pages

ROOM 34

The Book of Kells is one of the most famous European illuminated manuscripts. This thick book contains the four books of the New Testament, bound together in 680 pages of hand-drawn text and images. These four books are called the Gospels and tell the story of Jesus Christ's life. The Book of Kells is filled with neat rows of text as well as colorful designs that take up the whole page. All but two pages were painted!

PICTURING THE SAINTS

SAINT MATTHEW, BOOK OF KELLS, *c.*800 CE

Can you spot the hidden animals on this page? Look to either side of Saint Matthew, who is holding his gospel in the center. The animals here have special meanings. For example, the image of a peacock is thought of as a symbol of Christ. Here, there is a small calf on one side of his throne, which is a symbol for Saint Luke. On the other side is Saint John's symbol, an eagle. The Book of Kells was kept in the abbey of Kells in Ireland, until the Abbey was destroyed in 1641.

ART DETECTIVE

The Book of Kells was made by three artists and four scribes, all of whom were monks. One of these artists could illustrate in such fine detail that you need a magnifying glass to appreciate his work!

Medieval Europe 67

ROMANESQUE
Think Like the Romans

ROOM 35

The colorful Romanesque style began around 950 CE, more than 500 years after the fall of the western Roman Empire. It gets its name from the **Classical** Roman and Byzantine art that it was inspired by. Romanesque artworks include bright wall paintings and tapestries found in grand churches. Art from this time often includes the primary colors of red, blue, and yellow.

STICKS AND STONES
THE STONING OF SAINT STEPHEN, 1160s

Stephen was an early Christian who died when people who did not believe in Christianity threw stones at him. He was later made a saint for standing up for his beliefs. You can usually recognize him in paintings because he is shown surrounded by rocks. Paintings like these were often hand-painted on Romanesque church walls.

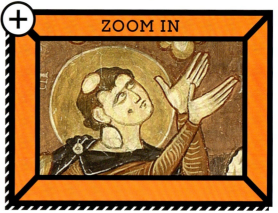

ZOOM IN

THE BATTLE FOR ENGLAND!
BAYEUX TAPESTRY, c.1066–82, NORMANDY

The Bayeux Tapestry in France is nearly as long as three tennis courts! It shows the Battle of Hastings in England, where the Norman people from France conquered England. The **tapestry** works like a long comic strip, unraveling the battle story as we go along. It is a highly detailed, and cleverly designed piece of embroidery using colored wool. In total, the tapestry has 626 people and 202 horses!

GOTHIC
The Grand Old Goths

ROOM 36

Gothic art is a style that developed from Romanesque art. The architecture is easy to spot by its pointed arches and giant stained-glass windows. Gothic churches were also decorated with sculptures all over the building, such as stone gargoyles along the rain gutters. In paintings, Gothic artists used lots of detail and depicted figures in a more lifelike way than is seen in earlier medieval art.

SCULPTURE EVERYWHERE!

ROYAL PORTAL, CHARTRES CATHEDRAL, c.1145–55

Grand reliefs surround Chartres Cathedral's entrance in France, bursting from its columns and doorways. The western walls alone hold 2,000 reliefs! Here in the portal we see Christ in the middle of the pointed space above the doorway. The row of figures below Christ are his twelve Apostles, or followers. The figures carved into the columns next to the door are people from the Old Testament of the Bible.

A COLORFUL CALENDAR

POL, HERMAN AND JEAN LIMBOURG LES TRÈS RICHES HEURES, c.1411/13–16

This is a page from a Book of Hours, which was a collection of popular books containing a calendar, prayers, and texts from the Bible. Many were filled with colorful illustrations, such as this picture of a New Year's feast for the month of January. The drawings in the stars at the top represent the month's zodiac signs of Capricorn and Aquarius, which are the star signs in January. The paintings in this book inspired the artwork in Disney's Sleeping Beauty!

GALLERY I
East Asia

East Asia is made up of China, Korea, and Japan. These areas were the home to some incredible inventions used in art, such as paper, silk, porcelain, and wood-block printing. Artists across the world today are still using the techniques perfected hundreds of years ago in East Asia!

The art found in ancient East Asian tombs tell us a lot about the early lives of people across the region. Some tomb art was small, like the guardian sculptures from Japan, but other examples are huge, like the terracotta warriors surrounding the tomb of China's first emperor.

Some of the rooms in this gallery also show religious art. You'll see Buddhist art from China and Korea, and art from Japan's native religion of Shintō.

Historians often organize artworks by the dynasties, or ruling families, who were in power at the time they were created. Each dynasty had its own preferences for art styles.

Continue ahead to see how East Asian cultures exchanged many ideas, while still creating incredibly unique artworks.

ROOMS 37–46

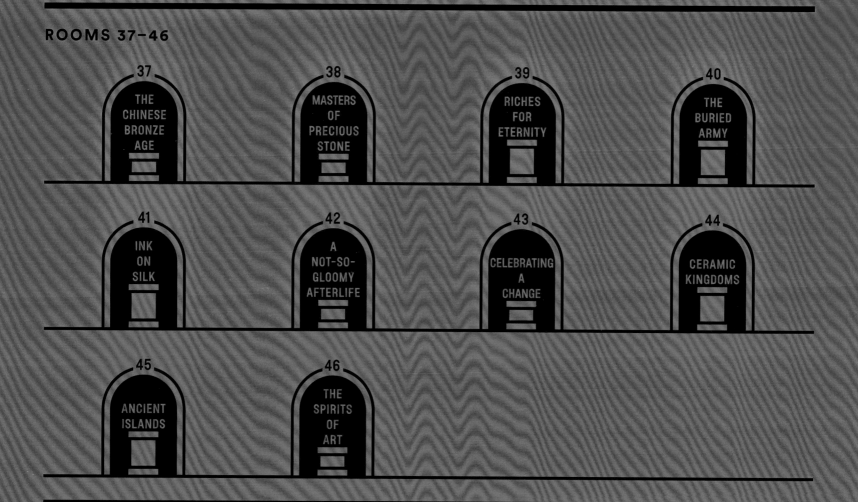

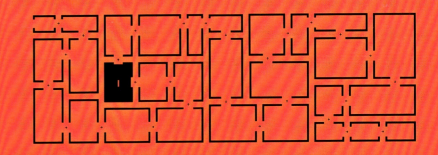

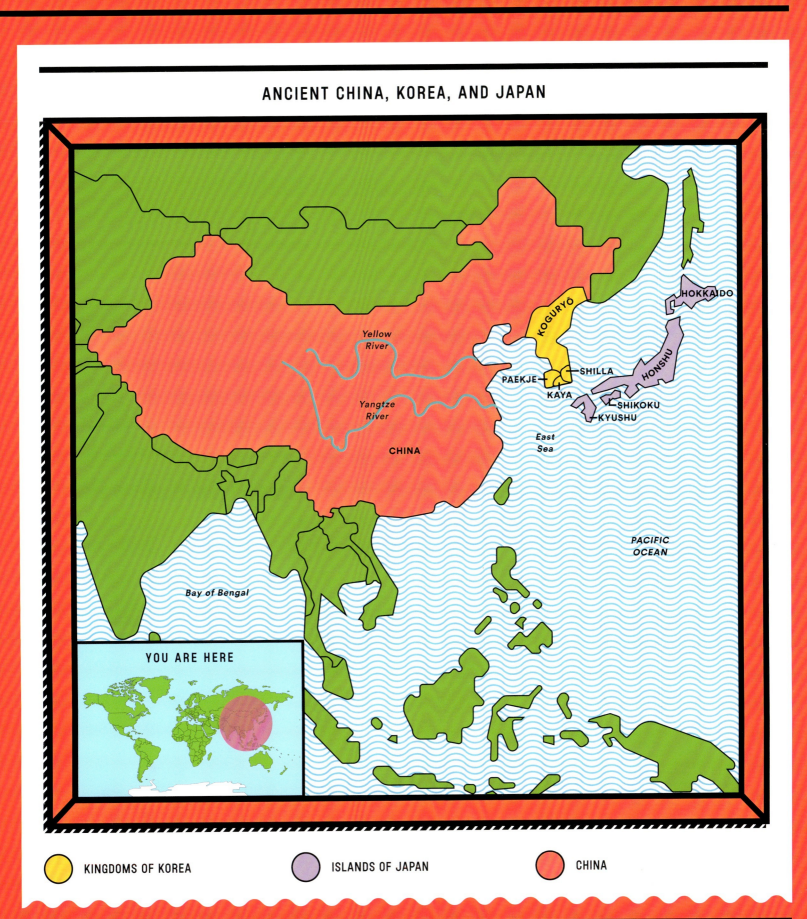

RITUAL BRONZES
The Chinese Bronze Age

The first Chinese dynasty (ruling family) was the Shang, which reigned from *c.*1600 to 1046 BCE. This dynasty settled along the banks of the Yellow River in northern China. There, people learned to mine copper and tin to make bronze objects, and this time is now known as the Chinese Bronze Age. Back then, people believed in a supreme god called Shangdi. They also prayed to their ancestors for good fortune using the bronze objects they made.

HIDDEN FACES
DING, SHANG DYNASTY, *c.*1384–1050 BCE

DRAGON DRINKS
FANG HU, ZHOU DYNASTY, *c.*500s BCE

Can you see a face on this pot? Many *ding* cauldrons have the faces of ancient creatures called *taotie* as part of their design. *Ding* bronzes could be used for both cooking and giving offerings. Families talked to the spirits of their ancestors by offering them food and drink in elaborate bronze containers.

👁 For more hidden faces in art go to pp.64, 90.

A *hu* is a wine container that could be placed in an ancestor's tomb or used in rituals. *Fang* means "square," so a *fang hu*, like this one, is a square-shaped wine container. The handles and feet are dragon designs. Traditionally, dragons were seen to have the power to control the rain. Farmers worshipped them in the hopes of bringing rainfall to their crops.

72 The Ultimate Art Museum

CHINESE JADE
Masters of Precious Stone

ROOM 38

Jade is a hard stone that was used to make jewelry, containers, religious objects, and more. As it is so hard, jade lasts a long time, but it is also very difficult to carve! To make a jade object, an artist had to drill and polish the stone many times. It was a very precious stone to the ancient Chinese. Jade is usually a shade of bright green but can also be orange, pink, brown, and purple.

THE PIG-DRAGON
COILED DRAGON PENDANT HONGSHAN CULTURE, c.4700–2900 BCE

HEAVEN AND EARTH
CONG TUBE, c.2500 BCE

The people of the Hongshan culture often buried their dead with these small jade objects. They are sometimes called pig-dragons because their heads are shaped a little like a pig. This is the earliest form of Chinese dragon designs.

👁 Dragons inspired art in lots of cultures! Check out pp.22, 60, 64, 65, 118.

The purpose of a *cong* is still a mystery! If you looked down at a *cong* tube from the top, it would look like a circle sitting inside a square. The circle shape represents heaven, and the square represents Earth. The outside of this *cong* tube has a *taotie* face design, an ancient creature in Chinese myth. It belonged to the Liangzhu culture.

East Asia 73

ROOM 39

OBJECTS FOR THE NEXT WORLD
Riches for Eternity

Wealthy people lived a comfortable life during the Han dynasty (206 BCE–220 CE) in China, and they didn't want that to end just because they had died! They wanted to take their land, servants, and belongings with them to the afterlife. The ceramic models found in the tombs of the Han and Tang periods (618–907 CE) show us what people thought was important to take into the next life.

A RICH AFTERLIFE

FUNERARY BANNER, MID-100s BCE

This painted **silk** banner was found in China in the tomb of an official's wife named Lady Dai. It was lying on top of a coffin that was tucked inside three more coffins. It is the earliest-known portrait and silk painting in Chinese art history. The middle shows pictures of Lady Dai being served by helpers and receiving gifts. The top section shows her in heaven with a snakelike dragon swirling around her. Between the painting and the luxurious treasures in her tomb, Lady Dai was sure to have a fabulous afterlife!

MOUNTED MUSICIANS

CAMEL WITH A BAND OF MUSICIANS, TANG DYNASTY, 618–907 CE

This ceramic burial sculpture shows a singer and a group of musicians riding a camel. Their instruments, such as the harp, oboe, and flute, are still used today. Camels were used along trade routes to carry goods across huge distances. This sculpture might be of foreign tradesmen from Persia who traveled to sell at the Chinese markets. Even people in the afterlife like to shop!

74 The Ultimate Art Museum

TERRACOTTA WARRIORS
The Buried Army

ROOM 40

In 1974, a group of farmers went out to dig a well in Xi'an, China, and accidentally discovered one of the biggest and grandest tombs in history! For hundreds of years, people shared wild stories about the tomb of the First Emperor of China, Qin Shi Huangdi (259–210 BCE). It turned out that the legends were true. The Emperor had more than 700,000 workers create life-size soldiers, horses, and chariots protecting a giant palace for his tomb.

READY FOR BATTLE
TERRACOTTA WARRIORS, *c.* 214 BCE

This sea of life-size warriors was originally painted in bright colors. Each one is unique and has the job of a real soldier in the Emperor's army. The soldiers carry weapons, such as crossbows, and are dressed ready for battle. There weren't just soldiers either. Some sections of this buried tomb include acrobats and an underground park complete with ducks for afterlife entertainment!

The figures are made up of separate parts that can be mixed and fitted together like puzzle pieces. The huge scale of this tomb shows the Emperor's obsession with living in luxury and conquering his enemies. So far he's done a good job. There is a river of highly toxic mercury trapped around his actual tomb, which means it remains untouched to this day.

CHINESE PAINTING
Ink on Silk

Paintings using ink on silk were popular in ancient China. In fact, silk was invented in China. Painters used pointed, tipped brushes made of goat, wolf, or deer hairs. The absorbent surface of silk did not allow for many mistakes, so artists had to know exactly what they wanted to paint before they started. Finished paintings were put on to scrolls on a wall or on handscrolls to be viewed on a table.

MAKING SILK
AFTER ZHANG XUAN, LADIES PREPARING SILK, EARLY 1100s CE

This is a copy of a lost painting from the Tang dynasty. Across the handscroll, the images show a group of palace women in the process of making silk. Can you see the different stages of the work?

This painting shows how long and difficult the process was! Across the country, there were workshops like this to make **textiles** by spinning, weaving, and dying the fabric.

ARTIST OR EMPEROR?
EMPEROR HUIZONG, AUSPICIOUS CRANES, 1112 CE

If something is "auspicious" it means that it is a sign that something good will happen. One day, clouds drifted over the Imperial Palace gates, and a group of cranes flew overhead in a strange pattern. Emperor Huizong, a painter and great lover of art, saw the cranes flying overhead, and took up his paintbrush! He made a poem and picture of the event, showing the birds swirling above the rooftops.

👁 The birds here symbolize good luck. There's another painting with flying birds on p.29. What do they symbolize?

KOREAN TOMB PAINTING
A Not-So-Gloomy Afterlife

ROOM 42

In ancient times, Korea was divided into several kingdoms. The largest was Koguryŏ, which is where the name Korea comes from. Korean artists studied writing and painting from their neighbors in China and mixed these with traditional Korean styles. Many of the earliest Korean paintings are found in the tombs of the rich and royal. The paintings show the life of Korean cultures long ago.

TOMB WITH A VIEW

HUNT SCENE, c.400–450 CE

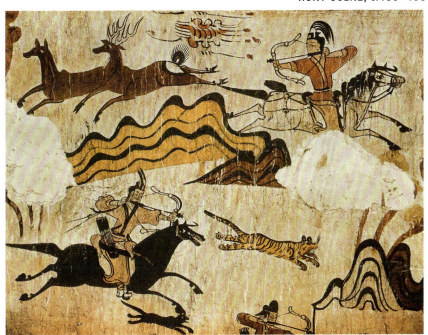

Both artworks on this page were found in the same tomb. Here we see figures riding on horses as they hunt deer and a tiger. The mountains in the landscape are shown as thick, wavy lines filled with color. These burial sites were so important that people began planning their tombs as soon as they got married!

ZOOM IN

DANCING FOR THE DEAD

DANCERS, c.400–450 CE

Want to see some ancient dance moves? On one end of this painting, a group of servants are bringing food to the deceased owner of the tomb. On the other end, a line of dancers raise their arms while doing a traditional Korean dance. Tomb paintings often showed people doing things they enjoyed when they were alive.

East Asia 77

ROOM 43

BUDDHIST SCULPTURE
Celebrating a Change

The Buddhist religion traveled thousands of miles along trade routes before reaching China in the Later Han period (25–220 CE). (To learn more about the story of Buddhism, see p.82.) The religion became so popular, it spread all the way across China to Korea, where the royal court converted to Buddhism in 372 CE. We can recognize the shift in beliefs through the bright paintings and sculptures that were made.

GLORIOUS IN GOLD

STANDING BUDDHA, 539 CE

This is the earliest example of Korean Buddhist sculpture. A swirling cloud showing that he is sacred surrounds the golden Buddha. His hand positions, called *mudras*, also have special meanings. The palm facing up means "do not have fear," and the palm facing down gives blessings.

CAVES OF A THOUSAND BUDDHAS

BUDDHIST SCULPTURES, TANG DYNASTY, 700s CE

In the year 366, a Buddhist monk had a vision that inspired him to place statues of the Buddha in a cave. Soon, others joined him, and eventually there were as many as a thousand caves full of artworks. The insides were decorated with Buddhist paintings and towering sculptures, and travelers between China and Central Asia stopped to visit. The site became a place for traders to meet and meditate near the important trading city of Dunhuang, China. When people traded less, the caves became buried under mountains of sand. They were rediscovered hundreds of years later in the early 1900s.

ZOOM IN

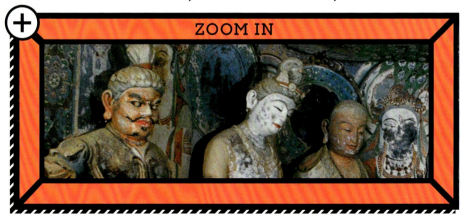

CHINESE AND KOREAN CERAMICS

Ceramic Kingdoms

ROOM 44

China and Korea are famous for their long tradition of ceramic art. Ceramics are made by shaping clay and baking it to make it hard. Different clays make different types of ceramics, such as the white porcelain invented in China. Glazes were added to give objects a shiny coating and color. The styles here were made with such great skill that nobody could recreate them (although they tried)!

RARE WARES

RU WARE BOTTLE, *c.*1075–1125

GREEN POTTERY

INCENSE BURNER, *c.*1100–50

Ware is another word for pottery. Ru wares were a special kind of pottery that were only made between 1086 and 1127 for the imperial court of China. Most of the Ru wares are pale blue, with lots of tiny cracks in the glazing. These cracks were not made on purpose, but people came to like them! Ru wares are very rare objects—there are only around sixty pieces left in the world.

There is a quick trick to tell that this ceramic object is from Korea—it's the color. Korean artists sometimes added iron oxide to their glaze, which made this soft green shade. This famous incense burner is in the shape of a flower. The feet are little rabbit designs. Burning scented materials was an important part of Buddhist rituals.

East Asia 79

ROOM 45

PREHISTORIC JAPAN
Ancient Islands

Before written history, the Jōmon culture lived on the islands of Japan. We know they lived there from the things they made. In fact, they are even named after the art they created. Jōmon means cord-making, a name which was given to them because of the ropelike designs on their pottery. A prehistoric period, called Kofun, is named after the tombs (*kofun*) built during this time, which were filled with protective figures and dishes.

CLAY MESSENGERS
SHAKŌKI FIGURE, *c.*1000–300 BCE

TOMB WARRIOR
HANIWA FIGURE OF A WARRIOR, *c.*500s CE

During the Jōmon period, people made little humanlike figures called *dogū*. As many as 15,000 *dogū* have been discovered. Here we see the style of the Kamegaoka culture—their style was to use large eyes, scrolling patterns on the body, and pointed legs and arms. It may have been used in part of a ritual to help people connect to the spirit world. The figure appears to be a woman, so some historians think they may be related to a Japanese mother goddess.

Haniwa are clay sculptures found outside of *kofun* or on mounds where people were buried. The name means "circle of clay" in Japanese because the first *Haniwa* were simple tubes. Warrior designs were more common in eastern Japan. This figure wears layers of armor and holds his sword at the ready to guard a tomb. It is such a fine example of a *Haniwa* figure that it is a national symbol for Japan.

80 The Ultimate Art Museum

SHINTŌ AND BUDDHIST JAPAN
The Spirits of Art

ROOM 46

Before the arrival of Buddhism between 538 and 552 CE, the main religion of Japan was Shintō, which means "the way of the gods." Shintoists believe that spirits called *kami* live in everything, even in art and buildings! At first there weren't many images of people in Shintō art. When Buddhist art styles later became popular in Japan, Shintō artists began to make more religious images and show *kami* as humans in art.

STORMS OVER KYOTO
LEGENDS OF KITANO SHRINE, c.1200–50

A shrine is a sacred or holy place. The Kitano Shintō shrine in Kyoto was built in 947 CE to please the angry spirit of Sugawara no Michizane, an official who had been unfairly exiled. When he died, the city of Kyoto suffered from sickness and terrible natural disasters. This painting shows Michizane as a storm god causing trouble before the shrine was built. The images are on a handscroll, which was unrolled in sections at a time and read from right to left.

THE TRAVELING PRIEST
KŌSHŌ, PRIEST KŪYA, c.1200–50

Kûya (903–972 CE) was a Buddhist monk who traveled around teaching people that they could live their next life in paradise if they chanted Amida Buddha's name. This lifelike wooden sculpture shows Kûya with six mini-Buddha figures coming from his mouth. They represent the chanting of Amida's name. The figure has crystals for eyes and was originally painted with color.

👁 The mini-Buddhas represent words. See p.196 for another way of using words.

ZOOM IN

GALLERY J
South and Southeast Asia

South Asia is the birthplace of Hinduism and Buddhism. Both religions inspired artists to carve giant sculptures into mountains and build temples from heavy stone! Here you'll find art about powerful beings that can create, destroy, or teach the world.

Hinduism is thought to be the world's oldest religion. It is different from many religions because it does not have a founder, but it does have many gods. In art, a lot of the Hindu gods are easy to recognize by their unique features, like Ganesha, who has the head of an elephant.

Buddhism also includes many divine beings called Buddhas. Buddhist philosophy began in India around 500 BCE. The real-life Buddha, Siddhartha Gautama, was born into a princely family in modern Nepal. As he grew older, he saw suffering in the world and decided to trade his royal life for a life of holiness.

South and Southeast Asia includes a lot of different countries, from India and Bangladesh to Indonesia! Over time, the Buddhist and Hindu religions spread throughout Asia and to parts of Europe, too. Step through the pages for a tour of the oldest religions and the art that celebrates them.

ROOMS 47–49

47 THE LIFE OF BUDDHA
48 THE FIRST HINDU ART
49 STUNNING STONEWORK

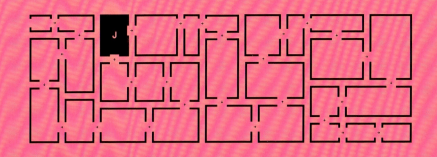
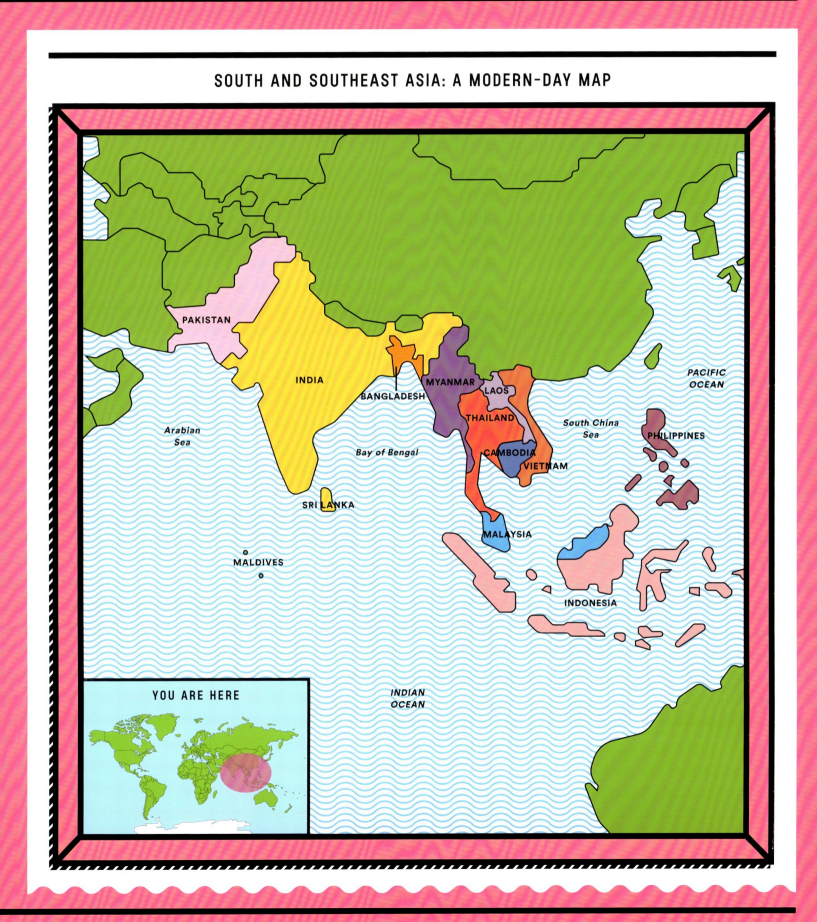

South and Southeast Asia 83

EARLY BUDDHIST ART
The Life of Buddha

When the Indian Emperor Ashoka (reigned 269–232 BCE) converted to Buddhism, he spread the beliefs throughout the Maurya Empire (modern-day India). Ashoka ordered artists to create thousands of artworks to help share Buddhist messages. Tall pillars were put up with writing carved on the sides, and huge mounds called *stupas* were built across the kingdom.

GLORIOUS GATEWAYS

NORTH GATEWAY, SANCHI, c.1–100 CE

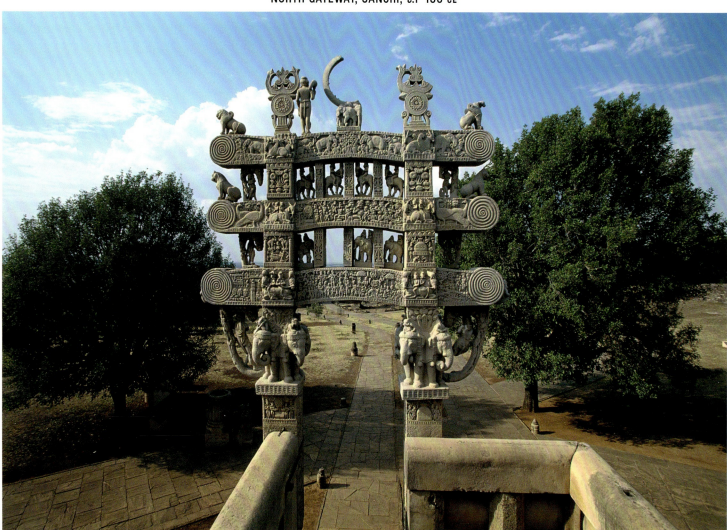

Stupas are big artificial hills made from dirt or stone. They hold important objects belonging to the Buddha or are located where a special event in the Buddha's life took place. The Great Stupa at Sanchi in India is one of the oldest Buddhist monuments. It is made of carved stone. Four gateways surround the *stupa*, pointing in the main directions of the compass. Each gate shows different stories from the Buddha's life.

? ART DETECTIVE

Images of the Buddha show him with very long ears. This represents the time he spent as a rich man wearing heavy earrings and reminds us that he left that life behind.

HINDU INDIA
The First Hindu Art

ROOM 48

The Hindu religion is more than 4,000 years old! Much of early Hindu art was made of materials that don't survive. Hindu art styles began to flourish during the Gupta Empire (320–550 CE), after Buddhist art. Under the Gupta dynasty, many temples and new styles of Hindu sculpture were created. Huge buildings, stone carvings, and paintings were made to share the religion across the empire.

GREATEST DREAM EVER
VISHNU ASLEEP ON THE SERPENT SHESHA, *c.*525 CE

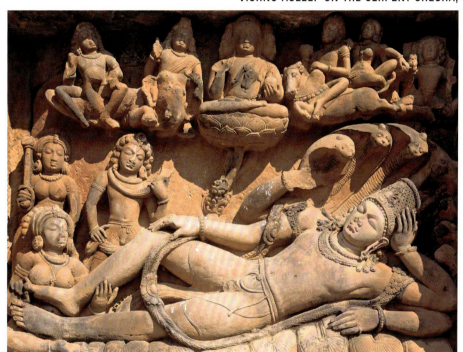

This is a carved stone panel from a temple. It celebrates the god Vishnu, who is protector of the earth. In this sculpture, Vishnu is creating the universe while he dreams. He is surrounded by other gods, including his wife Lakshmi, who is sitting by his feet. We can also see Shesha, the snake with many heads.

? ART DETECTIVE
Some Hindu gods have many heads to show they are powerful enough to face many challenges at once.

THE DANCING GOD
SHIVA AS LORD OF THE DANCE, *c.*1000s

Lord Shiva is the god of death and destruction, destroying evil and building the world new again. In this bronze sculpture, Lord Shiva dances, surrounded by a ring of fire, and tramples on a little figure that represents ignorance.

👁 Can you spot the four other pieces with dancers in this wing?

ELEPHANT IN THE ROOM
GANESHA, *c.*1300S–1400S

Here, Ganesha, the god of new beginnings, is sculpted from ivory. He is known to have a sweet tooth and is often shown holding a bowl full of sweets with his trunk stretched down toward the tasty treat. Can you see his stacked hairstyle? It is made to look like the temple roofs that were built at the time.

South and Southeast Asia 85

SOUTHEAST ASIAN ART
Stunning Stonework

ROOM 49

Southeast Asia stretches from Myanmar (or Burma) in the northwest to the Philippines in the east and down to Indonesia. The art in this huge area is wonderfully rich and varied! Early rulers had grand temples built to show off their power and celebrate their religious beliefs. Hindu and Buddhist temples included elaborate sculptures, stone reliefs, and colorful wall paintings.

TRAVELING KINGS
BOROBUDUR PANEL, LATE 700s TO EARLY 800s CE

Borobudur in Indonesia is the largest Buddhist temple in the world. It is decorated with detailed stone stories across its walls. Here, King Rudrayana, who became a Buddhist monk, is sending his ministers to build a new city. The detailed Indonesian ship also tells us how skilled they were at boat building many years ago!

THE DESTROYER DANCES
BHAIRAVA, c.1300

In Hinduism, Shiva can take the form of Bhairava, a fierce destroyer. He rides around on an equally fierce jackal! Statues like this were placed outside of temples or homes as guardians. They were also used in rituals to protect people from their enemies. Can you see all the deathly symbols in the stonework? Bhairava sits upon skulls and is even wearing a skull necklace and earrings. There is no mistaking that he is the destroyer. This statue is from east Java, Indonesia.

👁 Which ancient Egyptian goddess was also a protector and destroyer?

ZOOM IN

86 The Ultimate Art Museum

BE MORE LIKE BUDDHA

BODHISATTVA, LATE 1000s–EARLY 1100s

A Bodhisattva is someone who helps people to be more like Buddha. This wall painting is in the Abeyadana temple in the ancient city of Bagan, Myanmar. Unlike the wall painting in the Roman gallery (p.46), which was made on wet plaster, this fresco was painted on dry plaster. It is called a secco fresco. These types of fresco often don't last as long, especially in hot, humid climates, but the Bodhisattva we see here is a fine example that has lasted through the ages.

? ART DETECTIVE

Paintings in Buddhist temples often showed the many lives of the Buddha, while Hindu temples showed epic tales or stories from the ancient Hindu text the *Ramayana*. Telling religious stories through pictures was useful at a time when few people could read.

GALLERY K
Native Cultures of the Americas

From the native societies of the North American plains down to the chilly mountaintops of South America, this gallery is full of art from the first great societies of the Americas.

Native cultures are groups of people who were the first to live in a place. The first large civilizations in the Americas developed in Mesoamerica (meaning 'middle America') and in the Andes Mountains in South America around 5,000 years ago. Huge societies and empires blossomed in these areas, including the Olmecs, Maya, Inca and Aztecs.

There were also a great number of diverse societies living and making art in North America. Each culture had its own languages, beliefs and art practices. The makers in these different societies created objects using the natural resources that were unique to the areas they lived in.

From the 1600s, the story of native people across the Americas changed dramatically with invasions of European settlers. Many societies were lost or driven away from their land, but there are still artists working in some of these traditional styles today.

Get ready to explore the incredible early art of two huge continents as you open the door on to the last gallery of this wing…

ROOMS 50–55

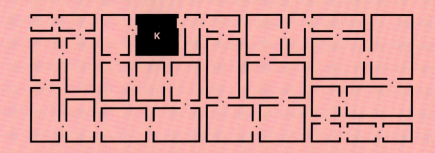
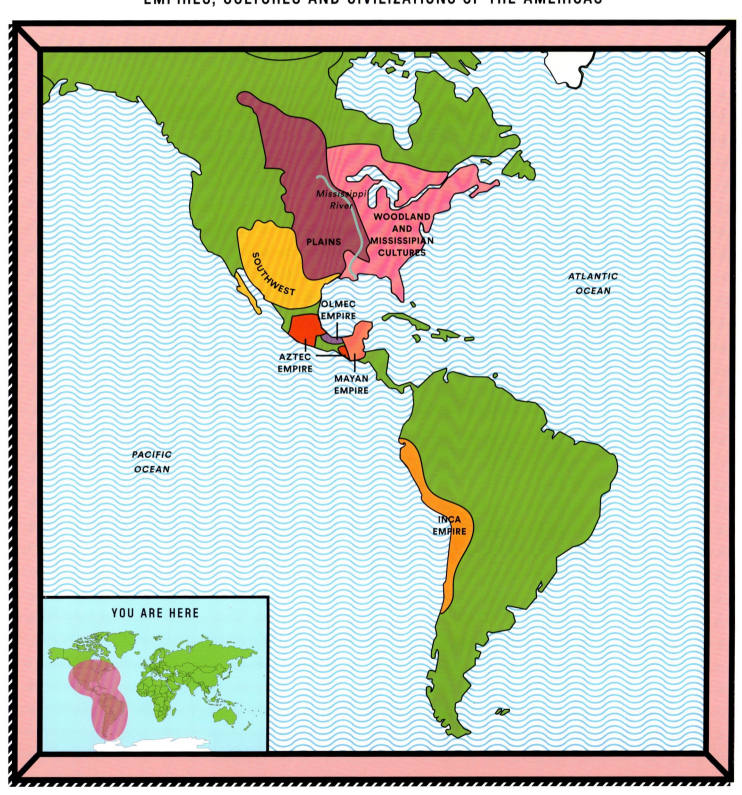

Native Cultures of the Americas 89

ROOM 50

THE SOUTHWEST AND PLAINS
Up and Down North America

Life could be tough in the southwestern deserts of North America. There were not many resources, so artists used what was available. Native cultures of the area, such as the Mimbres people, used clay for pots and instruments. Farther away, in the grasslands of the North American Plains, you'll discover stone carvings from the Dinwoody cultures in which the people used huge rocks as their canvas.

WRITINGS ON THE WALL
DINWOODY PETROGLYPHS, c.100–1400 CE

A petroglyph is another word for a rock carving. These are found in the Bighorn River Valley of Wyoming. Different people carved their own sections of these ancient designs over hundreds of years. Can you see the details in the lines? There is varying thickness as well as shading. This shows us some sophisticated carving techniques. Cultures living here also created textiles and wooden objects. These eventually decayed so are no longer around to learn from. Fortunately, we have their wall art!

BLACK AND WHITE ALL OVER
BOWL WITH BIRD AND FACE DESIGN, c.1050

The more you look at this bowl, the more you will discover! This style of black-and-white geometric pottery was made by the Mimbres culture in New Mexico. At the center of the design is a simple black face. Next to it, you can spot a white bird. These are both surrounded by a zigzag pattern that twists and cleverly mirrors itself.

> **? ART DETECTIVE**
>
> Some Mimbres bowls were used for burials. These usually had holes punched in the bottom and were placed over the faces of the dead.

90 The Ultimate Art Museum

WOODLAND AND MISSISSIPPIAN CULTURES

Ancient North America

ROOM 51

The first people came to North America between 30,000 and 15,000 years ago. Some moved east and grew into the Woodland cultures (c.7500–1000 BCE). Later, the Mississippian cultures took over much of the area around 900 CE. Their artwork shows what impressive builders and potters they were. Some of the art they made was even influenced by the ancient Maya culture of modern-day Mexico!

A LOVING MOMENT
MOTHER AND CHILD EFFIGY BOTTLE, c.1200

HAND OF POWER
EFFIGY HAND, 100 BCE–400 CE

This ceramic sculpture from a potter of the Mississippian culture shows a mother feeding her child. If you look closely around her neck and ankles, you can see the lines of her clothes, and the spread of her skirt underneath the baby. This vessel is from Cahokia, in Illinois, the largest Mississippian settlement. It is made from baked earthenware.

? ART DETECTIVE

The Hopewell Burial Mounds in southern Ohio are full of incredible objects! There are even fossilized shark teeth and spears made of **volcanic glass**.

The Hopewell peoples were a group of Woodland cultures who traded items, such as ceramics, and shared some common traditions, such as making art for funerals and rituals. Many Hopewell cultures created huge mounds, some of which were used as tombs. This long-fingered hand design was seen as a symbol of power. It was found in a burial mound in southern Ohio.

Native Cultures of the Americas

ROOM 52

THE OLMECS
Mysterious Rulers

The Olmecs (c.1400–400 BCE) were the first major civilization in modern-day Mexico. They invented their own calendar and hieroglyphics (a way of writing using pictures). Their art includes jade and ceramic figures, giant stone sculptures, and great pyramids with temples at the top. The Olmec's religion, inventions, and city plans went on to influence the Aztecs and Inca many years after they themselves had gone.

COLOSSAL CRANIUMS

PORTRAIT HEAD, c.1050 BCE

The Olmecs are famous for their gigantic stone head sculptures. Huge boulders were rolled down from mountains, pushed across rivers, then carefully carved. You would have to be pretty important to have a portrait this size! Historians believe these are stone portraits of the Olmec rulers. Seventeen have been found, and each one has unique facial features. This is another clue that the heads probably show real people and not gods. The helmets shown on these portraits were often worn during battles and traditional ballgames.

🔍 ART DETECTIVE

Maize, or corn, was important to the Olmec diet and led to the invention of popcorn!

92 The Ultimate Art Museum

CLASSIC MAYA ART
Fabulous Fans of Art

ROOM 53

The Maya civilization began around 1800 BCE and grew until the arrival of Spanish colonizers in the 1500s. The empire existed in present-day southern Mexico down to Honduras. They built sophisticated cities around towering pyramids and massive carved sculptures. Each city had its own king, and they were always competing with each other, so artists created portraits to show off a king's power!

POSH POTS
PAINTED VESSEL, c. 650–750 CE

LONG LIVE THE RULER!
PORTRAIT OF K'INICH JANAAB' PAKAL I, 615–683 CE

This Maya lord is getting all dressed up for a special dance. A servant is helping paint his body while he looks into a mirror. On the other side of the container, women are holding his mask and the staff he will use in a ritual. Painters were celebrated for their detail and skills. Earthenware pots like this would be decorated by an artist and given away as a gift to show off a person's wealth.

? ART DETECTIVE
Maya people ate chocolate and drank warm cups of cocoa. How do we know? Through images across their artwork! Their art shows us that this was an important part of their celebrations and rituals.

K'inich Janaab' Pakal I was a Maya ruler who reigned for nearly seventy years. That's the fifth-longest reign of any monarch in history! This sculpture was found in his tomb alongside small treasures, such and jade and pearls. Pakal's hair is designed like corn husks to show him as the maize god. Maize was very important to the Maya diet, so the maize god was one of the chief gods.

Native Cultures of the Americas

ROOM 54

THE AZTEC EMPIRE
Paradise on the Lake

The Aztecs (whose empire lasted from 1427–1521) didn't call themselves Aztecs but Mexica. The name Aztecs was assigned by historians. Their capital, Tenochtitlan (now Mexico City), was built on an island in a lake surrounded by volcanoes. It had canals and was dotted with towering temples. At the empire's peak, there was a wealth of poetry, pottery, sculpture, and objects made of precious metals, such as gold.

SIBLING RIVALRY
COYOLXAUHQUI SACRIFICIAL STONE, c.1469–81

This stone was at the bottom of some stairs that led to the temple for Huitzilopochtli, the god of war and of the sun. It shows his sister Coyolxauhqui, a Mexica moon goddess, who was angered when she learned that their mother was pregnant. She tried to lead her 400 brothers to a mountain to kill their mother but was defeated by Huitzilopochtli in a cosmic battle. She was sent crashing to the ground in pieces, just as we see in this disc.

👁 Can you find another sun god in this wing? Hint: look in gallery C!

FEARSOME FIGHTERS
EAGLE WARRIOR c.1482–86

This is a life-size sculpture of an eagle warrior. Eagle warriors, along with jaguar warriors, were famed for being the best in the Mexica army. They dressed like eagles, believing they would take on the bird's fierce hunting skills. This sculpture was placed outside the Templo Mayor, the Great Temple at the sacred center of the capital city. Sculptures like this were originally covered in feathers and painted in brilliant colors.

94 The Ultimate Art Museum

THE INCA EMPIRE
Makers in the Mountains

ROOM 55

The Inca Empire (1100–1533) once ruled over 12 million people stretching across the Andes Mountains in South America. Long roads connected cities, and caravans of llamas often clip-clopped along these routes.

Llamas were important animals for wool, food, and carrying loads. Much of Inca metalwork was taken and melted down by Spanish conquerors, but some textiles, containers, and sculptures still exist.

DRESS TO IMPRESS
ROYAL TUNIC, 1476–1534

AN ANCIENT HONEY POT
BOTTLE (URPU), 1450–1534

Tunics like this one were usually worn by important officials to show their allegiance to a ruler. The square geometric designs are called *tocapu*. See how detailed each square is? Every square tells a story about a person's role in society or where they came from. Textiles were typically made from cotton or llama wool. Wool from vicuña— a South American animal related to llamas— was particularly soft and special. It was forbidden for anyone but royalty to wear vicuña wool.

Urpu were storage containers for food and beer. This example is covered in rows and rows of bee paintings, so historians believe it may have been used to store honey. The small rings at the top were used for a lid, and the loops to the side helped with strapping it to transport (a llama). Inca pottery was used for practical or ceremonial purposes, such as offering food and drink to the gods or for feeding people in the afterlife.

Time for a snack!

Welcome to the Café

Take a seat, there's plenty of room. Browse through the menu, our artists have whipped up some delectable treats to tempt you.

Snacks

A FRUITY TREAT

PAUL CÉZANNE, STILL LIFE WITH APPLES AND ORANGES, *c.1899*

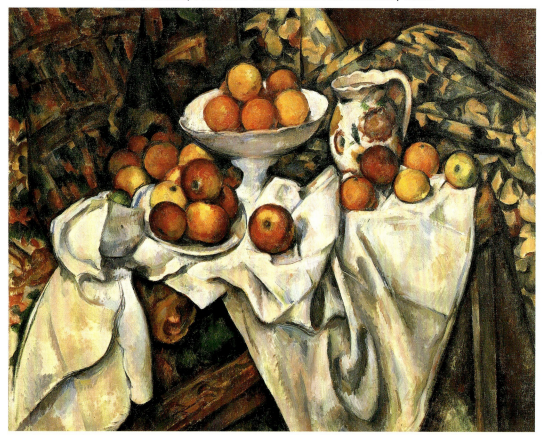

Enjoy apples from all angles! Cézanne painted tasty fruit to practice showing different sides of an object.

Mains

THE BIGGER THAN BIG BURGER
CLAES OLDENBURG, FLOOR BURGER (SOFT HAMBURGER), 1962

Warning! This giant sculpture is made of foam, not beef!

A PROPER FEAST
CLARA PEETERS, STILL LIFE WITH A TART, ROAST CHICKEN, BREAD, RICE AND OLIVES (c.17TH CENTURY)

A mouth-watering painting that looks real enough to eat.

Dessert

FRUIT SURPRISE!
GIUSEPPE ARCIMBOLDO, VERTUMNUS, 1590

Having fun with food makes it twice as good.

TREAT YOURSELF
WAYNE THIEBAUD, TWO LEMON MERINGUE PIES, 1983

Pies and ice cream are Wayne Thiebaud's specialty!

WING

2

MASTERING THE ARTS

STEP INTO A NEW PERIOD IN ART HISTORY.

Prepare to meet some superstars of the art world!

In wing one, a lot of art was made for the rich and powerful, and we don't know who made much of it. In this wing, individual artists became famous for their skills, and more people had money to buy art. This meant artists could show subjects that ordinary people liked, such as scenes from everyday life. The invention of the printing press also made it easier to print and share ideas through books.

INSIDE THIS WING YOU WILL DISCOVER...

- The Renaissance
- Amazing Landscapes
- A Pottery War
- Powerful Portraits
- Epic Tales
- Illustrated Books
- Oil Paintings
- Hidden Messages
- Sacred Sculptures
- A Volcanic Eruption
- Drama!
- Dreamy Scenes
- Stunning Still Lifes
- Easter Island Sculptures
- Royalty and Rulers
- Masks

GALLERY L
Arts of Asia

This gallery will explore great masterpieces from the 1200s to the 1800s. From the deserts of Persia (modern Iran) to the islands of Japan, these unique artworks tell incredible stories through paintings, textiles, and even puppets!

In the 1200s and 1300s, huge empires were growing and changing across Asia. The Mongol Empire became the largest ever geographically unbroken empire in history. This meant you could have walked from China to modern Poland in Europe without ever leaving its lands! In India, the Mughal Empire ruled much of South Asia from the 1500s to the 1800s. Through art, we can see how the people across these empires shared many ideas.

Many of the countries were also connected by the Silk Road. It was not actually a road made of silk, but a name given to routes people used for travel and trade. People shared materials, ideas, and art styles along these roads. Some techniques and subjects used by artists might be similar, but the way these great artists used them was unique to their culture.

Get ready to explore artworks filled with color and incredible details...

ROOMS 56–64

56 TINY WORLDS
57 EVERYDAY ART
58 SCHOLARLY PAINTINGS
59 HISTORY AND HOME
60 PERFECT PORCELAIN
61 FOLD IT CAREFULLY
62 A STORY OF COURT LIFE
63 BRILLIANT BUILDINGS
64 WOVEN WONDERS

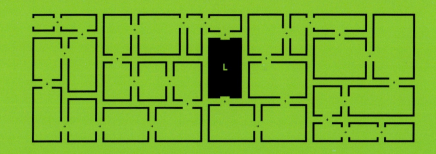

THE COUNTRIES OF ASIA AND THE SILK ROADS

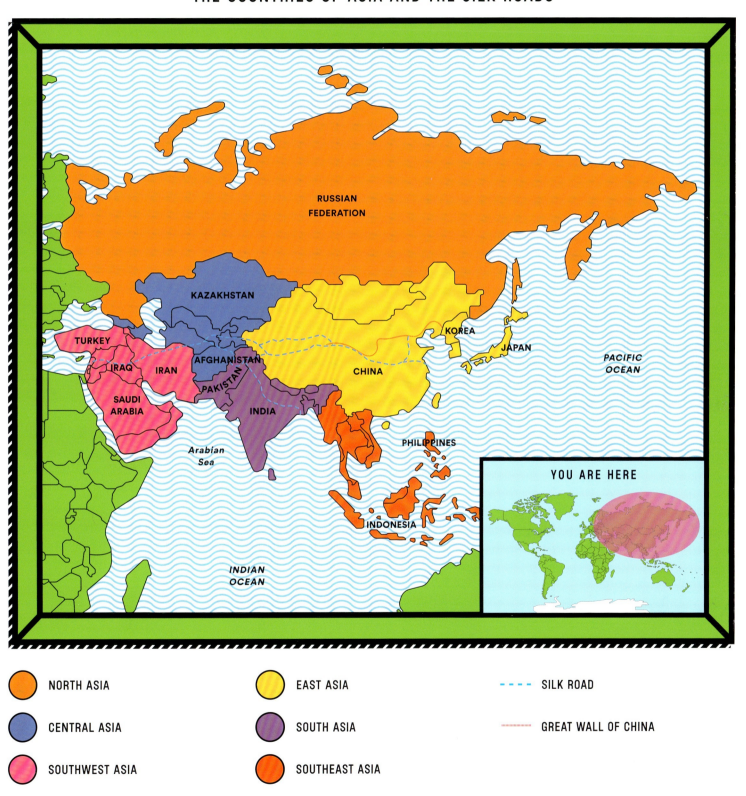

- 🟠 NORTH ASIA
- 🟣 CENTRAL ASIA
- 🩷 SOUTHWEST ASIA
- 🟡 EAST ASIA
- 🟪 SOUTH ASIA
- 🟧 SOUTHEAST ASIA
- ---- SILK ROAD
- ——— GREAT WALL OF CHINA

Arts of Asia 101

ROOM 56

MINIATURE PAINTING
Tiny Worlds

Do you know why these paintings are called miniature? Because they are very small and packed full of tiny details. They are so small that some artists used mini-paint-brushes made with squirrel hairs! The earliest Indian miniature paintings were created in the 800s CE as pictures to illustrate

102   The Ultimate Art Museum

Buddhist and other religious texts. During the Mughal Empire (1526–1858), more studios were created for miniature painting. Artists started using this style to paint different stories and images from history, royal life, and more.

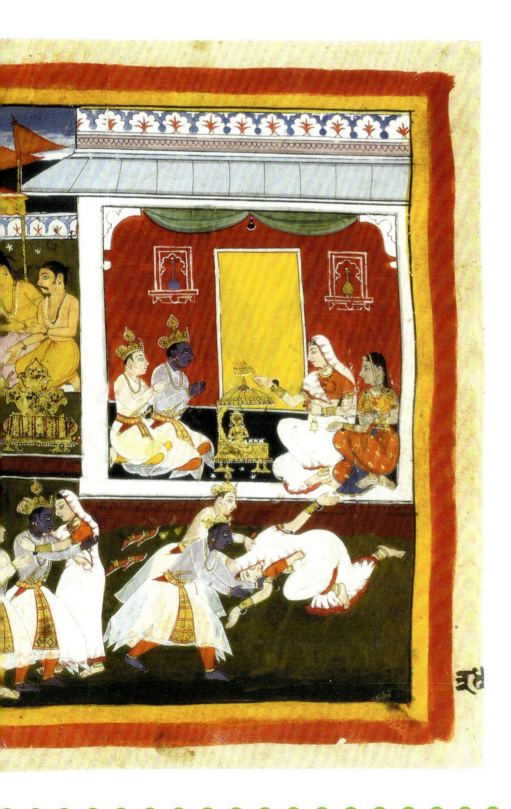

ART IN VERSE

SHAHIBDIN, RAMAYANA, c.1650

The *Ramayana* is an epic poem (a long story told through poetry) that tells of a legendary prince named Rama. It's one of India's oldest and most loved stories! It includes the story of Rama and his beautiful wife, Sita, as well as a powerful monkey god named Hanuman, and a battle with an evil king named Ravana. Plus, Rama is not only a prince, but also a human incarnation of the god Vishnu. This painting is by the Muslim artist Shahibdin, who painted many Hindu subjects. Do you see how the blue figure of Rama appears more than once? The painting is showing multiple scenes within one picture. It shows the moment that Rama's stepmother kicks him out of the kingdom to live in the forest with Sita. At the bottom right, you can see his mother falling to the ground as she hears of the news. This painting is taken from a copy of the *Ramayana* that includes 450 paintings. Although one person wrote the text for the manuscript, groups of painters worked together to make the colorful pictures. It took five years to finish!

👁 Miniature painting traditions have inspired some modern Indian artists. Take a look on p.180.

Arts of Asia 103

THE ELEPHANT TAMER

BASAWAN, AKBARNAMA, c.1590

Akbar was one of the great rulers of the Mughal Empire, which stretched across much of South Asia, including modern India and Pakistan. Akbar reigned during the 1500s for nearly 50 years. Even though he could not read, he supported many writers and artists by establishing workshops at which they could create art. This page is part of an illustrated book telling the story of his reign. It shows the Emperor in white, riding one of the more unruly royal elephants named Hawa'i. He bravely charges after a rogue elephant while everyone else appears terrified! This picture and story are shown to demonstrate Akbar's power and ability to tackle difficult things, such as ruling a big empire.

How did other rulers in history show their power through art? Check out pp.21, 31, 48, 52, 75, 92.

DECORATIVE ARTS
Everyday Art

ROOM 57

There is a term for art that is found in our everyday lives. It's called decorative arts. These are objects that people use but that are also wonderful pieces of art to look at. It can include pottery, jewelry, a carpet, and more. Traditional decorative arts in Southeast Asia include fabrics, furniture, and even puppets. Artists use local materials, such as bamboo and coconuts, to create masterpieces with a purpose.

SAILING INTO THE AFTERLIFE
PALEPAI SHIP CLOTH, 19TH CENTURY

PUPPET'S PLAY
WAYANG GOLEK PUPPET, BEFORE 1881

A *palepai* is a woven cloth that hangs behind people during ceremonies. If you're getting married, you hang a palepai cloth. Naming a new baby? Hang a palepai cloth. Many of these cloths have ship designs on them, as they are connected to the people on the Indonesian island of Sumatra. This particular cloth would have been used for a funeral, since the belief is that when someone dies, they go into the afterlife on a ship.

👁 To see another culture where ships were important and also depicted in art, go to p.36.

This is an Indonesian *wayang golek*, which is a wooden puppet on a rod. The heads are carved and painted, and the clothes are made from real cloth. Puppet shows are usually held for special events, such as weddings and festivals. This puppet represents Kencana Wungu, Queen of the Hindu kingdom of Majapahit.

Arts of Asia 105

CHINESE PAINTING
Scholarly Paintings

ROOM 58

Powerful Mongolian warriors once conquered China and started the Yuan dynasty (1279–1368). This upset many Chinese officials (scholars), who chose to retire instead of work for the new rulers. They lived quiet lives and used paintings to show how they felt. These are called scholar paintings. Later Ming and Qing dynasty art includes scholar paintings of nature, plants. and animals, as well as grand royal scenes.

LETTING GO

DONG QICHANG, EIGHT SCENES IN AUTUMN, 1620

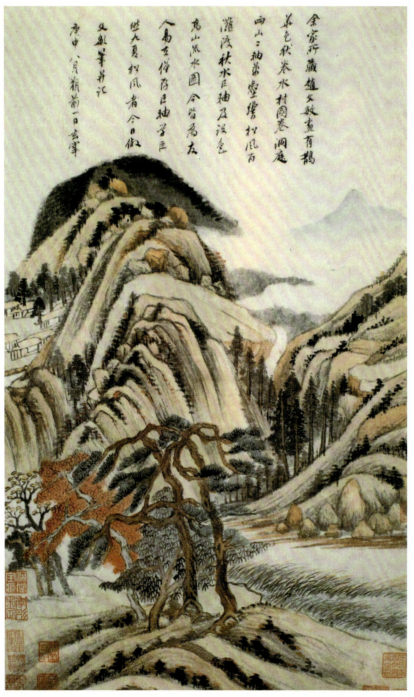

Dong Qichang was a highly respected scholar painter. He studied hard to become an official in the Ming court, but he often found reasons to leave and visit his home in what is now Shanghai. While there, he wrote poetry and painted. He felt many artists were painting in an orderly way, using too many details and tiny brushstrokes, and he wanted to do something different. Dong preferred a relaxed style of brushstroke that was closer to ancient Chinese painting. He also thought it was more important for a painting to show a mood than it was to show a lifelike version of a scene. This painting shows impossible views of the tops and sides of mountains at once, with trees that are much too big. To him, it was more important to clearly show the cheerful colors in nature as the leaves change in autumn than to be realistic.

ART DETECTIVE

Scholar-officials (also called *literati*) were people who worked for the government. They studied for a long time to pass a difficult test to get a job working for the court. As part of their studies, they learned about music, writing, and painting.

MIGHTY BAMBOO

GUAN DAOSHENG, BAMBOO AND STONE, 1262–1319

Guan Daosheng was an accomplished painter and poet. Some say she is one of the most famous women painters in Chinese history! Guan was a master at painting images of bamboo. These plants are a symbol of strength in Chinese painting because bamboo stalks stand strong, even in the cold and wind. This was a popular theme during the Yuan dynasty, as it encouraged scholars to stay strong under Mongol rule.

🔍 ART DETECTIVE

Many plants in Chinese ink paintings can have special meanings. There are four plants known as the Four Gentlemen, which each represent the seasons of the year: spring (orchid), summer (bamboo), autumn (chrysanthemums), and winter (plum blossom).

HORSING AROUND

ZHAO MENGFU, HORSE AND GROOM, 1296–1359

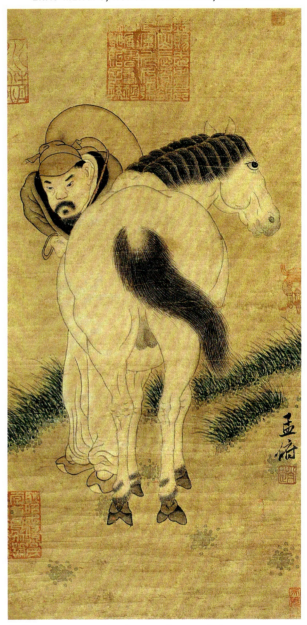

While many scholars rejected the new Mongol rulers, the scholar painter Zhao Mengfu chose to work with them to represent traditional Chinese ideas in their court. He is well known for his paintings of horses, which could have different meanings. This ink painting offers a rear view of a horse and its caretaker. Showing a horse and groom could represent how the government should choose good officials, like a groom picks a good horse. The way Zhao uses his brushstrokes gives the grass and hair a lifelike appearance.

Arts of Asia 107

ROOM 58

THE GREAT TOUR

WANG HUI, THE KANGXI EMPEROR'S SOUTHERN INSPECTION TOUR, SCROLL THREE: JI'NAN TO MOUNT TAI, *c.*1698

During the Qing dynasty, China was ruled by the Manchus, who came from northeast China. One of the Qing emperors, known as the Kangxi Emperor, lived in Beijing in the north, but he wanted to show his power across all of the great lands of China. The Kangxi Emperor and his family took a 2,000-mile tour across southern China, and he asked the landscape painter Wang Hui to record the trip in pictures. Wang is one of the most celebrated landscape painters in Chinese art. This is one of twelve long scrolls showing the journey. This painting shows the Kangxi Emperor at Mount Tai, a sacred mountain visited by emperors since before 200 BCE. Tiny figures are dotted throughout this craggy mountain scene. Yellow was a color only worn by the Emperor. Can you find him?

Arts of Asia 109

KOREAN PAINTING
History and Home

ROOM 59

During the early Chosŏn dynasty (1392–1910), Korean artists were inspired by Chinese styles, particularly the scholar paintings, which you'll notice in the first room in this gallery. But from the 1700s, Korean artists decided to focus on different styles—ones that were unique to the history and traditions of Korea. Paintings didn't only show landscapes, but also scenes that were relatable to everyday life.

QUIET THOUGHTS

KANG HŬIAN, A SAGE CONTEMPLATING THE WATER, 1400s

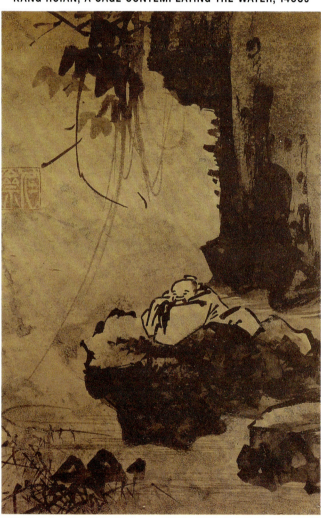

The artist Kang Hŭian was a well-known scholar and court official. He had traveled to Beijing, China, for his work and was inspired by the scholar paintings he'd seen there. In this scene, a scholar rests his chin on his folded arms and looks down into a pool of water. Perhaps he is thinking of something important, or simply daydreaming peacefully. Wispy black lines overhead show the twigs and branches of a tree, and straight gray lines at the bottom show the ripples in the water.

TRUE VIEWS

CHŎNG SŎN, MANP'OKDONG, c.1750

In the 1700s, an artist came along who wanted to try something different. Instead of painting **idealized**, imaginary places, Chŏng Sŏn walked outside and painted the real Korean landscapes and city views that he saw. These were true to the way Korea really looked, so this style is called 'true-view' landscapes. Other artists were quickly inspired by his new approach and started to create Korean paintings in this style.

110 The Ultimate Art Museum

CHINESE AND KOREAN CERAMICS
Perfect Porcelain

ROOM 60

The ceramics from China and Korea were uniquely beautiful, and people across Asia and Europe loved them. Other countries tried to copy the Chinese technique for making bright, white porcelain, but it was a guarded secret. Korean artists mastered their own ceramics techniques with a traditional pottery style called *punch'ŏng*. The Korean artists were so skilled that entire villages of potters were kidnapped in war!

BLUE AND WHITE ALL OVER
DAVID VASES, YUAN DYNASTY, 1351

This pair forms one of the earliest examples of Chinese blue-and-white porcelains. They were inspired by bright blue ceramics from the Islamic world and were originally made for trade with those countries. The shape of the vases is a similar style to some ancient bronzes (see room 37). What mythical creatures can you spot here? Dragons and phoenixes are often shown together as symbols of yin-yang (balance), an idea that comes from an ancient Chinese philosophy called Daoism.

WARE WARS
PUNCH'ŎNG WARE BOTTLE, 1400s

Imagine pottery that was so well loved that people fought a war over them! That's just what happened with the punch'ŏng wares from Korea. During the 'Pottery Wars' between 1592 and 1597, many Korean potters were taken as prisoners by the Japanese to make ceramics in Japan. The ceramics were made by covering wares with a slip (liquefied clay) that had lots of iron in it, then covering that with a smooth coating called a glaze. When they were fired in the oven, they turned a soft green color, just like this example.

Arts of Asia 111

JAPANESE SCREENS
Fold It Carefully

ROOM 61

Japanese folding screens can be used to divide rooms, as backgrounds during ceremonies, or to provide privacy. They were made with silk in ancient times, but when artists started using paper in the 1300s, the styles changed. Artists first created single-color designs. Then from the 1500s, screens covered with brilliant colors and glittering gold artwork became popular and showed people's wealth.

MISTY MOUNTAIN
KANŌ TAN'YŪ, LANDSCAPE WITH MOUNT FUJI, 1666

For over 300 years, the Kanō family and their students created the most influential painting styles in Japan. Kanō Tan'yū is a famous artist from this group because of the works he painted for the shogun (the military ruler). This screen shows the volcano Mount Fuji in the cloudy distance, with hills to the front. This is called a *yamato-e* image, which shows recognizable scenes from Japan.

BRISTLING BRUSHES
HASEGAWA TŌHAKU, PINE TREES IN MIST, 1550–1600

This is one of two matching screens by Hasegawa Tôhaku. Both show pine trees in a misty landscape. The soft shades of the trees almost look like shadows behind a lit screen. The artist used a brush that was not too wet to create rough brushstrokes that look like pine needles. He studied the styles of Chinese and Japanese painting masters, and studied under the famous Kanō family of artists in Kyoto.

THE TALE OF GENJI
A Story of Court Life

ROOM 62

The Tale of Genji is an epic story with more than fifty chapters and over 400 characters! It explores the life of handsome official Hikaru Genji and is thought to be the world's first novel. The author was a Japanese woman named Murasaki Shikibu (c.973 CE–1015). Artists began to paint scenes from her tale in the 1100s. They often show scenes by painting buildings from a high angle and without the roof, so we can see the people inside.

WIND THROUGH THE WINDOWS
SCHOOL OF TOSA MITSUYOSHI, "NOWAKI," (CHAPTER 28), EARLY 1600s

Between patterned clouds covered in gold leaf, this scene shows Genji's wife Murasaki as she watches her servants try to close window blinds against typhoon winds. The artist of this work is believed to have painted in the workshop of the famed painter Tosa Mitsuyoshi, who came from a family of artists who created the Tosa school. It wasn't an actual school, it is just a way of describing artists who work in similar styles.

LOVE AND GAMES
"MURASAKI" AND "UTSUSEMI" (CHAPTERS 3 AND 5), 1600s–1800s

During a time in Japanese history called the Edo period (1603–1868), *The Tale of Genji* was a popular subject on prints, paintings, and folding screens. Courtiers and wealthy people loved to see images of the court life from the book. This paper screen shows the main character, Genji, when he sees the beautiful girl Murasaki. Eventually, they fall in love and marry. At the bottom, we see Genji again. He's standing in the doorway watching his stepmother and another woman play a board game called *Go*.

ZOOM IN

Arts of Asia 113

MUGHAL ARCHITECTURE
Brilliant Buildings

During the Mughal dynasty, new buildings combined Indian, Persian, and Turkish architectural styles in a grand new way. The buildings are often symmetrical, which means that if you imagine drawing a line down the middle, they'd look the same on both sides. Many also include rows of pointed arches and large onion-shaped domes on top. Royal tombs are some of the best examples of this style, and the Taj Mahal is the most famous of all.

AN AMAZING MAUSOLEUM
USTAD AHMAD LAHAURI, TAJ MAHAL, 1632–53

The Taj Mahal is a magnificent white marble building in the city of Agra, India. It looks as impressive as a palace, but it is actually a mausoleum, which means it's a house for a tomb. The emperor Shah Jahan (1592–1666) had it built in memory of his dearest wife, Mumtaz Mahal, when she died. The Taj Mahal is so grand that it took 20,000 people and 22 years to build! The outside of the main building is decorated with Arabic script from the Qur'an and curling floral patterns made from many colorful stones, including lapis lazuli, jade, amethyst, and more. It was built along the Yamuna River and has beautiful gardens, fountains, and pools at the front. Mumtaz Mahal's marble tomb was placed inside, and another one for Shah Jahan was added later when he died, so the two could rest side by side.

CARPETS FROM THE ISLAMIC WORLD
Woven Wonders

ROOM 64

Just like ancient stories, carpet designs were also passed down between generations of weavers over hundreds of years. Designs could be simple or have complex geometric, floral, and animal patterns, depending on the village or country where they were made. Carpets for royal courts were made with elaborate decorations and expensive materials, such as silk, as a show of wealth.

AN ENORMOUS CARPET
MAQSUD OF KASHAN, ARDABIL CARPET, 1539–40

The Ardabil Carpet is huge—it's about half the length of a tennis court! We know the age of this carpet because of the writing along the edge. It says that it was made by an artist named Maqsud Kashani between 1539 and 1540. Other inscriptions quote poetry from the Persian writer Hafiz. The center of the carpet has a large golden medallion surrounded by decorative ovals, two lamps, and a sea of floral designs. This carpet was made for the shrine of Safi al-Din Ardabili (1252–1334) in the town of Ardabil, Iran. He founded the Persian Safavid dynasty and was a Sufi saint.

👁 How does this compare to the carpet on p.122?

🔍 ART DETECTIVE

From the 1500s, rulers of the Ottoman, Safavid, and Mughal empires created workshops to make and sell carpets to European buyers. These became popular luxury items across Asia and Europe, and they even show up in some European paintings. They were considered such precious works of art that some people hung them on the wall rather than laying them on the ground! Renaissance paintings are a great way to see carpets that are no longer around.

Arts of Asia 115

GALLERY M
The Renaissance in Europe

The word *renaissance* means "rebirth." This was an exciting time in Europe, when artists studied cutting-edge science and rediscovered Classical (Greek and Roman) ideas. What they learned was combined and "reborn" into something new.

Across Europe at this time, people were full of questions. How does the human body work? How could materials, like paints, be improved? What art techniques looked most realistic? All of that curiosity led to some big changes. Artists came up with better ways to mix oil paints and began to paint on canvas for the first time. And what scientists learned about the human body helped them paint and sculpt people who looked very real.

The subjects of artworks changed a lot as well.

Leaders from the Catholic Church paid artists to paint Christian stories, but more people outside of the Church started to have money for art too. They asked their favorite artists to make paintings and sculptures for their houses that showed portraits, mythology, and everyday life. This is how skilled artists such as Leonardo da Vinci and Jan van Eyck became so well known. Get ready to discover some of the most famous artworks in the world!

ROOMS 65–70

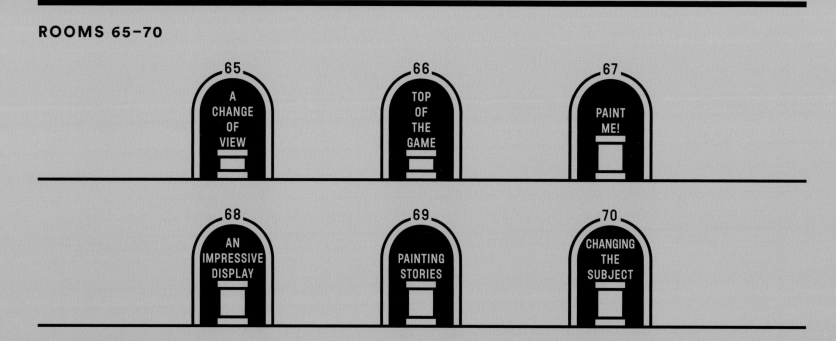

65 A CHANGE OF VIEW
66 TOP OF THE GAME
67 PAINT ME!
68 AN IMPRESSIVE DISPLAY
69 PAINTING STORIES
70 CHANGING THE SUBJECT

116 The Ultimate Art Museum

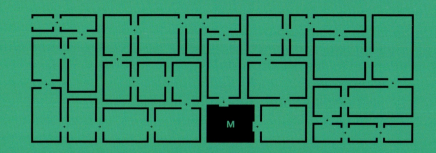

FROM MIDDLE AGES TO MODERNITY: EARLY MODERN EUROPE, 1559

---- HOLY ROMAN EMPIRE

QUATTROCENTO
A Change of View

ROOM 65

Quattrocento is short for *millequattrocento*, which is Italian for "the 1400s." It's the name given to art made during this time. Quattrocento artists kicked off the Renaissance period in Florence, Italy.

Some artists experimented with **perspective**. That's where they change the position and size of objects based on how faraway they are, so they look more realistic. This idea would become huge in European art!

A GARDEN IN SPRING
SANDRO BOTTICELLI, PRIMAVERA, c.1478

Botticelli—the name of the famous artist who painted this work—was actually a nickname. Botticelli—meaning "little barrel"—came about because the artist was smaller than his rounder, older brother, known as "barrel"! Botticelli lived in Florence all of his life, though he was paid to paint works for the Pope in Rome as well. He is famous for creating detailed and dramatic paintings of myths and religious stories. The title of this painting, *Primavera*, means "spring." It shows the Roman goddess Venus in the middle, and the god Mercury on the left. Flora, the goddess of spring, is shown in a flowery dress.

DRAGON SLAYING
PAOLO UCCELLO, SAINT GEORGE AND THE DRAGON, c.1470

The dragon in this painting doesn't stand a chance against Saint George! Paolo Uccello painted the legendary knight driving his spear into the beast to save a princess. Uccello was also a keen mathematician, interested in learning how to use perspective in paintings to make them more realistic. He tried to achieve it by making the rectangular patches of greenery pinch together as they move toward the background. He also angles the lines on the ground to look like they are going into the distance.

👁 How does this dragon look compared to the Chinese dragon on p.111?

DEFEATING A GIANT
DONATELLO, DAVID, c.1460s

BREAKING BOUNDARIES
PROPERZIA DE' ROSSI, RELIEF OF JOSEPH AND POTIPHAR'S WIFE, c.1520s

It was no easy task being a woman sculptor during the Renaissance, a time when people thought that sculpting was something for men only. Properzia de' Rossi proved them wrong! She first discovered her love for sculpture by carving tiny works into the stones of fruit like apricots and peaches. Later, she created larger works in marble for churches. This relief was originally made for San Petronio, a church in Bologna, Italy. It shows Joseph from the biblical book of Genesis running away from his master's wife.

Donatello began his career creating sculptures for cathedrals in Florence. He studied the Classical sculptures of ancient Greece and Rome, and tried many different styles. Some of his sculptures are carved from wood, and others—such as *David*—are similar to the smooth bronze statues of ancient Greece. This sculpture shows David after he had slain the giant Goliath in the famous Bible story.

? ART DETECTIVE

Properzia de' Rossi was the only woman artist with a chapter in the first edition of *Lives of the Most Eminent Painters, Sculptors, Architects*. This was a book published by the artist Giorgio Vasari in 1550. He wrote about 142 artists and is sometimes called the first art historian.

The Renaissance in Europe

ROOM 66

HIGH ITALIAN RENAISSANCE
Top of the Game

The High Renaissance is called "high" because it is when the **movement** was at its peak. The new artistic styles that had started in Florence spread to Rome and then on to other areas of Italy. This was Renaissance art at its best! These artists brought Classical (Greek and Roman) ideas about learning, intelligence, and being an individual into their art. This mash-up of new and ancient styles brought the beauty of their world to life.

AN ELEGANT ERMINE

LEONARDO DA VINCI, LADY WITH AN ERMINE (CECILIA GALLERANI), 1489–90

Leonardo da Vinci was extremely curious and clever. He dreamed up ideas for flying machines, sketched detailed pictures of the human body, designed military equipment, and still found time to paint some of the most famous images in the world! This oil painting is of a woman connected to the Sforza family, who ruled the Italian state of Milan. The weasel-like animal she's holding is called an ermine. Da Vinci thought of them as pure creatures.

👁 Can you spot two other portraits with pets in this gallery?

GREAT MINDS

RAPHAEL, SCHOOL OF ATHENS, 1509–10

In this fresco, Raphael painted a gathering of great mathematicians, scientists, and thinkers from ancient Greece. Raphael created this work to celebrate the brainiacs of the ancient world, which was a popular topic at the time. In reality, these people would have never met because many (such as Aristotle and Pythagoras) lived at different times. As models for these ancient philosophers, Raphael used geniuses from his own time. In the center, wearing purple and red, is Leonardo da Vinci as the philosopher Plato. The artist Michelangelo is in the front (resting his head on his hand) as another great thinker, Heraclitus. Raphael's painting is also an excellent example of perspective! Take note of how the archways in the hall grow smaller as they go back.

👁 Artists got better and better at painting perspectives. Go to p.118 to see how it started.

THE GIANT SLAYER

MICHELANGELO, DAVID, 1501–04

Michelangelo was an artist of many talents, celebrated for his painting and sculptures. He was so well loved that he became the first **Western** artist to have a biography written about him while he was still alive. Michelangelo's enormous *David* was carved for Italy's Florence Cathedral. It was meant to go high up in a church, but when officials saw the finished work, they thought it deserved to go in the town square. Like the artist Donatello (see p.119), Michelangelo was inspired by ancient Greek sculpture and used this style in his artwork. Here, he draws on the biblical story of David and Goliath. David is holding a slingshot to take down the giant Goliath.

ART DETECTIVE

From the time Michelangelo trained as an artist, he sculpted and painted many artworks for the Medici family. They were bankers and merchants who became rich and ruled Florence for nearly 300 years. They were also great art lovers. They purchased art by Raphael, Botticelli, Leonardo da Vinci, and many other artists. Their family eventually became very powerful across Europe and included four Popes and two French queens! Michelangelo's *David* was not made for the Medicis, but they did own Donatello's *David* in room 65.

FAMILY TIME

LAVINIA FONTANA, PORTRAIT OF BIANCA DEGLI UTILI MASELLI WITH HER SIX CHILDREN, c.1565–1614

Lavinia Fontana was one of the first women in Europe to make a career as an artist. She supported herself and her family with the sales from her paintings, and her husband worked as her assistant. In her early career, people from her hometown of Bologna came to her for portraits, and soon her reputation grew throughout Italy. She even painted works for the court of the Pope, including the Pope himself. This family portrait shows a noblewoman with her six children and their pets. The five sons wear the same fabric, but the daughter wears a unique pattern. The details of their **embroidered** clothes show how special the fabrics must have been in real life.

The Renaissance in Europe

NORTHERN RENAISSANCE PORTRAITS
Paint Me!

ROOM 67

The Northern Renaissance includes artists from the Netherlands, Flanders (modern Belgium), and Germany. They were inspired by Italian artists and Gothic art, but wanted to make their work even more lifelike. Their discovery of better ways to mix paint helped. Thick oil paints allowed artists to show tiny details and build up layers of color. The paintings were so realistic that more people bought portraits for their homes.

A ROYAL PORTRAITIST
HANS HOLBEIN THE YOUNGER, THE AMBASSADORS, 1533

Hans Holbein the Younger was known for his incredibly realistic portraits. He was also one of King Henry VIII's favorite artists. This painting shows two French ambassadors surrounded by symbols of heaven and Earth. If you look at the painting from a certain angle, the log-like shape at the bottom becomes a skull.

ZOOM IN

MARRIED LIFE
JAN VAN EYCK, GIOVANNI ARNOLFINI AND HIS WIFE, 1434

The Netherlandish artist Jan van Eyck was a master at showing lifelike details with oil paints. This double portrait shows a wealthy married couple. They are most likely in their home and are shown with their dog, which is a symbol of loyalty. A self-portrait of van Eyck can be seen in the mirror on the back wall. He used layers and layers of paint to show the colors of the skin and the textures of the different items in the room in a realistic way.

122 The Ultimate Art Museum

A MOODY SELFIE

ALBRECHT DÜRER, SELF-PORTRAIT, 1500

The German painter and **printmaker** Albrecht Dürer traveled around Europe gathering inspiration from Northern European and Italian artists. He studied how to paint people and use perspective in his paintings. This dark self-portrait shows the artist at 28 years old, in a style similar to many paintings of Christ.

ART DETECTIVE

Albrecht Dürer often put a symbol of his initials on his artworks so that people knew they were by him. As his pictures became popular, some artists copied the "AD" symbol to sell their own works. He once had to take an artist to court to make him stop!

AN ARTIST AT WORK

CATHARINA VAN HEMESSEN, SELF-PORTRAIT AT THE EASEL, 1548

This is the earliest example of a self-portrait in which an artist shows themself in the act of painting. The Flemish artist Catharina van Hemessen painted herself wearing a nicer dress than she would have really worn while working. These clothes are to show her high position in society. The writing at the top tells us that she was 20 years old in this picture. Van Hemessen most likely learned to paint with her father, by helping him with religious pictures. Later, she progressed to painting small portraits of women. People were amazed at the lifelike quality of her portraits, and soon she was making works for important patrons, including the Governor of the Netherlands, Mary of Hungary.

Can you find five other paintings in this wing that show artists while they are painting or drawing?

The Renaissance in Europe

NORTHERN RENAISSANCE ALTARPIECES
An Impressive Display

An altarpiece is an artwork that sits behind a table (the altar) at the front of a Christian church. It can have one or more paintings or sculptures and is sometimes divided into many sections. Altarpieces usually show scenes from the Bible. Northern European altarpieces often have a set of panels joined together that can be folded closed. The backs of the panels are also painted, so that they are still eye-catching when closed!

UP TO NO GOOD

HIERONYMUS BOSCH, TRIPTYCH OF THE HAYWAIN c.1500–05

Hieronymus Bosch's paintings were very imaginative. He painted fantastical landscapes filled with people and made-up creatures. The Triptych of the Haywain shows the story of humans across three panels (a triptych is an artwork with three parts). The left shows the creation of humans according to the Bible. The center shows people behaving badly, which leads on to the frightful afterworld in the right-hand panel. There are snake-people, winged rats, and other wild creatures throughout the scenes!

ZOOM IN

124 The Ultimate Art Museum

THE GHENT ALTARPIECE

JAN AND HUBERT VAN EYCK, ALTARPIECE OF THE LAMB, 1423–32

The twelve scenes of this huge altarpiece don't always continue across panels, and the figures are also different sizes from scene to scene. For these reasons, historians think it's possible that the panels weren't originally made to be part of the same altarpiece. The detailed scenes are bursting with a mix of activities. The top panels show the Virgin Mary, Christ, and John the Baptist, but other sections show an organist and portraits of real people from van Eycks's time. It is considered one of the best examples of colorful, lifelike Northern Renaissance painting.

👁 Can you find the other artwork by Jan van Eyck in this gallery?

ART DETECTIVE

This altarpiece in Ghent, Belgium, has been through a lot. It was almost destroyed in a fire in the 1500s, and it has been stolen more than any other artwork in history. It was once stolen by Napoleon's army during the French Revolution and displayed in the famous Louvre Museum in Paris. In 1934, the bottom right panel, called *The Just Judges*, was stolen, and it's still missing to this day. The panel you see here is a copy. The most recent theft was in 1942, when the Nazis stole the altarpiece during the Second World War. They hid it in salt mines, and it wasn't found again until 1945.

The Renaissance in Europe

HISTORY PAINTING
Painting Stories

ROOM 69

History paintings show historical, religious, mythological, and popular stories. These often show dramatic moments, and artists use their imagination to paint scenes with an honorable message. From the Renaissance to the 1800s, artists felt that history paintings were the most important subject to paint! They were followed by portraits, genre painting (see opposite page), landscapes, animals, and then still lifes (objects).

DON'T ANGER A GODDESS
TITIAN, DIANA AND ACTAEON, 1556–1559

Titian is one of the great masters of the Italian Renaissance. He started studying painting at the age of ten and created more than 600 works over his lifetime! He painted portraits and landscapes, but he is best known for his colorful history paintings of religious and mythological scenes. This painting shows the hunter Actaeon stumbling upon Diana, the Roman goddess of hunting, while she is bathing with her servants. Diana is shown wearing a tiara, to the right, as a woman quickly covers her. Diana is so furious about Actaeon's interruption that she turns him into a stag. If you look on the column to the left of Diana, you can see a stag skull, which is the artist's clue to Actaeon's fate.

126 The Ultimate Art Museum

GENRE PAINTING
Changing the Subject

ROOM 70

For a long time in Europe, paintings were paid for by churches and the government. They wanted artists to make paintings to teach the Bible and show examples of good behavior. But as more people started to read, their knowledge grew and they wanted art about other topics! Genre paintings show moments of everyday life. They became very popular and were often made small enough for people to hang in their homes.

PAINTING IN RIDDLES
PIETER BRUEGEL THE ELDER, NETHERLANDISH PROVERBS, 1559

Pieter Bruegel the Elder painted scenes from everyday life, including the daily lives of peasants. His paintings were very different from the history paintings (see opposite page) and grand portraits other artists were making at the time. Each one is packed with busy activities, from doing laundry to playing games. Here, Bruegel uses a village scene as a creative way to illustrate old Netherlandish sayings. Can you see the man running into a brick wall to the lower left? This demonstrates the saying, "don't bang your head against a wall," which means trying to do an impossible thing. The painting is full of more than 100 little riddles like this, waiting to be solved!

The Renaissance in Europe

GALLERY N
European Painting 1600-1850

This is an exciting time in Western art history! Artists were perfecting their skills and making new rules they would eventually break. They started to ask questions about what stories art could tell.

As we grow and learn, the things we find stylish often change. When you were younger, you probably liked a lot of toys that you don't like so much anymore. Between the 1600s and mid-1800s, there were changes like this in art. Artists created new "movements," which is when a group of artists work in a similar art style that looks different from what came before. In this next set of rooms, you will see many movements established by artists with different opinions about how art should look.

But artists are always learning and changing, just like you. The twists and turns of this gallery will show you how art styles can shift in a very short period of time. Sometimes there were even several movements happening at once! Get ready for a whirlwind tour of incredible movements in art…

ROOMS 71–77

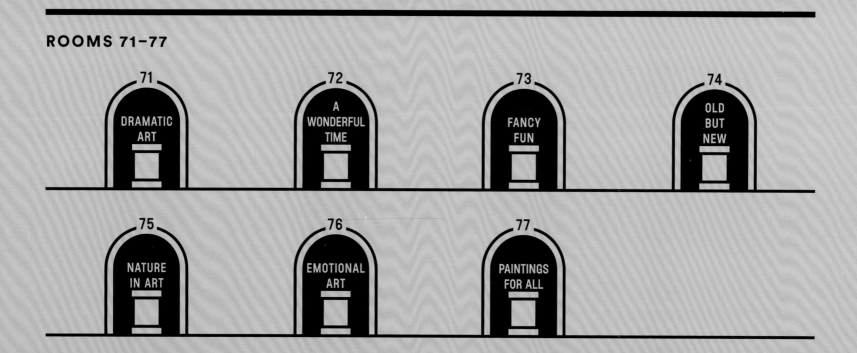

71 DRAMATIC ART
72 A WONDERFUL TIME
73 FANCY FUN
74 OLD BUT NEW
75 NATURE IN ART
76 EMOTIONAL ART
77 PAINTINGS FOR ALL

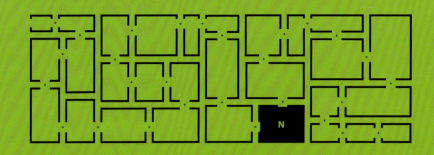

EUROPE IN 1815

European Painting 1600–1850

BAROQUE
Dramatic Art

ROOM 71

The Baroque style started after 1545, when the Catholic Church wanted paintings that looked lifelike and dramatic. They hoped these artworks would promote Christian ideas. To make scenes moodier, artists painted dark shadows and highlighted areas to look like they were lit by a candlelight. Even artists who weren't painting for the Church started to create art in this style. European art became more dramatic than ever before!

PAINTING A PRINCESS
DIEGO VELÁZQUEZ, LAS MENINAS, 1656

Diego Velázquez was an official painter for the Spanish royal court and is famous for his portraits. In *Las Meninas*, Velázquez shows himself painting in his art studio inside the Royal Palace. The room includes the *Infanta* (Spanish princess) Margaret Theresa and her many servants. Did you notice that everyone is looking out at you? It's like you're part of the painting! If you were actually in the room, you would be standing in the position of the king and queen, who are reflected in the mirror at the back.

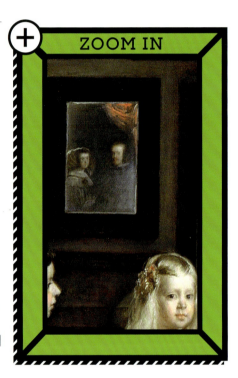

ZOOM IN

OVER THE EDGE
ELISABETTA SIRANI, TIMOCLEIA KILLING THE THRACIAN CAPTAIN, 1659

When a Greek soldier harmed and tried to rob a woman named Timocleia, she tricked him by flipping him into a well and throwing stones on his head. The Italian artist Elisabetta Sirani painted many scenes like this, showing women as brave leaders. She also taught other women painters.

A MAD GENIUS
MICHELANGELO MERISI DA CARAVAGGIO, BOY BITTEN BY A LIZARD, 1595–1600

Michelangelo Merisi da Caravaggio was a rascal of the art world. He got into fights and had a rotten temper, but people still bought his work because they loved the way he showed emotional expressions and dramatic lighting. The boy's face here shows the pain of a lizard bite!

A BAD HAIR DAY

PETER PAUL RUBENS, SAMSON AND DELILAH, c.1609

Peter Paul Rubens is famous for his history paintings using rich colors and showing people striking lively poses that feel full of energy. This painting shows Samson, a biblical figure known for his incredible strength. But there was a catch to his powers—his strength came from his long hair! Here Rubens shows the moment when Delilah—the woman he loved—betrayed him by cutting his hair while he was sleeping.

ART DETECTIVE

The technique of contrasting bright highlights and dark shadows to make scenes extra dramatic is called **chiaroscuro**. It was used by many Baroque artists. *Chiaro* means "light" and *scuro* means "dark" in Italian.

SLEEPING GODS

ARTEMISIA GENTILESCHI, VENUS AND CUPID, c.1625–27

Artemisia Gentileschi grew up studying painting under her father, Orazio Gentileschi, in Rome. After moving to Florence, she became hugely successful by selling her dramatic history paintings. Many of her paintings showed strong heroines standing up to men, but this one shows the Roman goddess of love, Venus, having a nap with her son Cupid nearby. It was likely to have been made as a request for an important buyer.

Cupid and Venus were popular subjects in art. To see more works where they feature, go to pp.45, 49, 118.

DUTCH GOLDEN AGE
A Wonderful Time

ROOM 72

A golden age is a great time to be alive! In the 1600s, the Dutch had one such age. They were among the best tradesmen, scientists, and artists in the world. Dutch artists used the realism and drama of the Baroque style, but didn't just stick to religious subjects. They were especially fond of genre (see room 70) and **still life** paintings, which could be packed with hidden meanings and new techniques to show off their skill.

FLOWERS THAT LAST
RACHEL RUYSCH, STILL LIFE WITH FLOWERS AND FRUIT, 1707

Painting still lifes of food and flowers were all the rage during the Dutch Golden Age. Painters such as Rachel Ruysch could show their skill in painting textures and great detail. Ruysch's father studied plants, so from a young age she learned to arrange and paint flowers. She used dark backgrounds in her paintings, which helped the colorful flowers stand out. Hidden among the blossoming petals and spiraling vines in her paintings, you can also find beetles, butterflies, and other insects.

👁 Can you find another Dutch still life in the café?

PAINTING ABOUT PAINTING
JOHANNES VERMEER, THE ART OF PAINTING, c.1666–68

Johannes Vermeer often painted scenes that included sunlit windows. This light would stream into the scene and brighten the figures within. Do you see the gentle ripples in the wall tapestry and the gleam on the chandelier? This painting shows off Vermeer's skill for painting light, shadows, and the way they look on different surfaces. The floor pattern also shows his great understanding of perspective because he had to adjust the shapes of the checked tiles to show them going further back into the room.

👁 Can you find one other chandelier in this wing?

THE IMPORTANCE OF LIGHT
REMBRANDT VAN RIJN, THE NIGHT WATCH, 1642

A MUSICAL PAINTING
JUDITH LEYSTER, BOY PLAYING THE FLUTE, 1630

When Rembrandt van Rijn wasn't busy making up to 100 self-portraits, he was a very popular painter for wealthy clients in Amsterdam. *The Night Watch* is a huge painting that looks like a historical scene, but it's actually a group portrait. It shows a military force in action. These were groups of men who could be called upon to defend a city or stop riots. Rembrandt paints the leaders with light shining on them so they stand out from the other figures of the group. Light is a good way for artists to show who is important in a painting and where we should focus our attention.

ZOOM IN
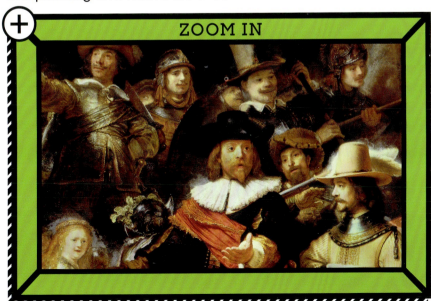

This young boy looks so lifelike, you can almost hear his flute! Judith Leyster painted many lighthearted genre scenes of smiling people playing music and games. She was so skilled that she was accepted as a member of the famous Guild of St. Luke in Haarlem, Netherlands. She was one of the first women in the guild. Certain jobs, like being a painter or doctor, once required people to join a guild before being allowed to work. After joining, Leyster ran her own painting workshop, teaching other artists. Before the 1600s, working in a workshop was the way most artists learned their craft. Although she was a successful artist during her lifetime, Leyster's importance was forgotten for a long time after she died. This is because some of her paintings were mistakenly thought to be by other artists, such as her husband, Jan Molenaer, working in a similar style.

👁 Can you find 11 other women artists in this wing?

ROCOCO
Fancy Fun

ROOM 73

Rococo is all about fun! Before the Rococo movement in France, King Louis XIV built the grand Palace of Versailles and made his royal court live there. He also made many not-so-fun rules about how people should behave and how art should look. When he died, everyone was free to live how they wanted to again! Artists created the Rococo style, showing the new leisurely, carefree life of the French upper class.

A POPULAR PORTRAITIST
THOMAS GAINSBOROUGH, IGNATIUS SANCHO, 1768

The English painter Thomas Gainsborough loved to paint landscapes, but supported his family by selling portraits. This is the only known portrait of Ignatius Sancho, a writer, composer, and abolitionist (someone who wants to get rid of slavery). When they first met, Gainsborough was painting portraits for the family Sancho worked for as a servant. He completed this painting in just an hour and forty minutes! Gainsborough went on to become a founding member of the Royal Academy in London, and Sancho became the first Black man to vote in a British election.

PORTRAITS IN PASTELS
ROSALBA CARRIERA, SELF-PORTRAIT, 1715

In the 1700s, portraits drawn with pastels became hugely popular, thanks to Rosalba Carriera. Pastels are similar to crayons, except the pigment is mixed with oils or gum instead of wax. This creates a soft, chalky look. Carriera started her career by making small portraits in Venice, where tourists liked them so much that she was able to move to Paris for more work. Her clients included the French royal family and nobles from across Europe. In this painting, Carriera shows herself drawing a portrait of her sister and assistant, Giovanna.

SUGARY SWEET SCENES

JEAN-HONORÉ FRAGONARD, THE SWING, 1767

This dreamy scene is painted in soft, cotton candy colors that are very common in Rococo art. It shows an upper-class couple having fun in the woods. The woman kicks so high as she swings that her shoe has flown off! Jean-Honoré Fragonard is known for his romantic scenes of couples.

PARTY IN STYLE

JEAN-ANTOINE WATTEAU, THE EMBARKATION FOR CYTHERA, 1718

When Jean-Antoine Watteau studied at the French Royal Academy, his paintings were so unique that the academy created a new category for them. They were called *fêtes galantes* (charming parties), and typically show wealthy people enjoying themselves. The painting shows the island of Cythera, home to the goddess of love, Aphrodite, in Classical myths. The blue paint he used was a newly invented color called Prussian blue. This blue pigment was much cheaper than others made from more expensive pigments, such as the lapis lazuli stone.

➕ ZOOM IN

➕ ZOOM IN

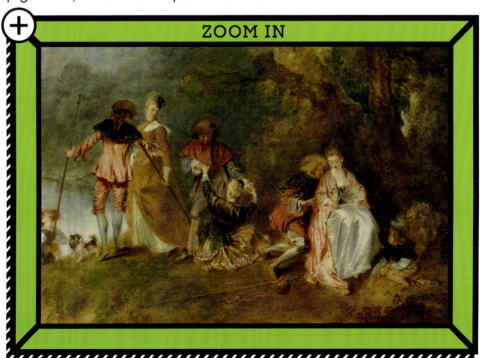

NEO-CLASSICAL
Old but New

ROOM 74

Neo is the Greek word meaning "new." *Classical* describes ancient Greek and Roman art. So Neo-Classical is a new version of Roman and Greek art styles! The movement began in the 1700s, as artists traveled more around Europe. They were fascinated by the myths, as well as the rediscovered artworks from ancient Roman cities that had been buried in volcanic ash. These artists used Classical styles and stories to make new art.

NAPOLEON AS A GOD
JEAN-AUGUSTE-DOMINIQUE INGRES, NAPOLEON I ON THE IMPERIAL THRONE, 1806

Jean-Auguste-Dominique Ingres studied art under the leading artist of Neo-Classicism, Jacques-Louis David (see opposite page). This portrait of Emperor Napoleon Bonaparte is inspired by famous artworks, such as an ancient statue of the Greek god Zeus. The pose is similar to a painting of God by Jan van Eyck (see p.125).

A FASHIONABLE QUEEN
ELISABETH LOUISE VIGÉE LE BRUN, MARIE ANTOINETTE WITH A ROSE, 1783

The Neo-Classical style became popular during the reign of King Louis XVI and Queen Marie Antoinette of France. The queen loved fancy dresses and sometimes wore hairstyles as tall as a small child! She especially liked paintings by Elisabeth Louise Vigée Le Brun and asked her to create more than 30 portraits of her and her children. This work shows the queen wearing fine silks to support French silk weavers. Vigée Le Brun painted more than 600 portraits and 200 landscapes, with clients including royalty and famous actors and writers.

IMAGINING ERUPTIONS

JOSEPH WRIGHT OF DERBY, VESUVIUS FROM PORTICI, 1774–76

Joseph Wright of Derby's paintings of volcanoes were so bright and dramatic that people could imagine just how hot lava and rocks might look spewing from a mountain! Wright visited Naples, where Mount Vesuvius is located, but never witnessed the mountain erupt. Vesuvius is the infamous volcano that erupted over the city of Pompeii nearly 2,000 years ago. The ash that covered the city helped preserve the mosaics and wall paintings you can see in the Roman gallery (see p.46).

DUTY, HONOR, REVOLUTION

JACQUES-LOUIS DAVID, THE OATH OF HORATII, 1784

The leader of the Neo-Classical style was Jacques-Louis David. He made works to support the French Revolution and later painted heroic portraits of Emperor Napoleon Bonaparte. Much of his work shows stories from Classical mythology but ties them into what he thought about the French government. This painting shows the ancient Roman legend of three brothers who bravely went to war to serve Rome. The scene symbolizes loyalty to one's country.

A PAINTING ABOUT DRAWING

ANGELICA KAUFFMAN, DESIGN, c.1778–80

In this painting, Angelica Kauffman shows a figure drawing a sculpture to represent the idea of "design." Many artists learned to draw at this the time by sketching sculptures for practice. Kauffman was one of two women in the group of artists that founded the Royal Academy of Arts in London in 1768.

ART DETECTIVE

Starting in the 1600s, attending **art academies** became a more common way for artists to train. Neo-Classicism was the preferred style in art schools for many decades.

European Painting 1600–1850

PAINTINGS OF THE LAND AND SEA
Nature in Art

ROOM 75

For hundreds of years, European academies taught artists that landscapes were less impressive subjects than history paintings. But some artists carried on painting them. From the late 1700s, artists such as J. M. W. Turner and John Constable painted landscapes and seascapes that were so unique, people really took notice! More artists developed their own landscape styles, and they too became popular.

MOODY CLOUDS
JOHN CONSTABLE, A RAIN STORM OVER THE SEA, 1824

There are two main themes to remember in John Constable's work: landscapes and clouds. The British artist painted and sketched many clouds, showing the ways they drifted and how different they could look in various kinds of weather. This image shows dark lashings of gray and black over the sea. From the lines and direction of the brushstrokes, it's clear that Constable is showing a terrible rainstorm.

👁 If you like storms, take a look at the painting of a storm in this museum's garden on p.155!

AMERICAN LANDSCAPES
ROBERT DUNCANSON, BLUE HOLE, LITTLE MIAMI RIVER, 1851

It was not only European artists who were creating incredible landscape paintings. American artists like Robert Duncanson traveled to Europe and were inspired by the epic nature paintings they saw there. Duncanson was a free Black-American landscape painter working during the time of slavery in the United States. He was part of the Hudson River School, which was a movement and not actually a school. These artists painted grand landscapes of American scenery—especially of towering mountains and winding rivers. Duncanson painted this peaceful section of a river near his family home in Ohio in more than one painting.

138   The Ultimate Art Museum

A MODERN AGE

J. M. W. TURNER, THE FIGHTING TEMERAIRE, TUGGED TO HER LAST BERTH TO BE BROKEN UP, 1838

Joseph Mallord William Turner became a student at the Royal Academy in London when he was only 14 years old! Throughout his career, he liked to take his art supplies outside and paint in nature—no matter the weather or time of day. There's even a story that Turner had himself tied to a ship during a storm so he could experience the waves. The brushstrokes in his paintings are intentionally messy, and he often used vibrant colors that showed how sunlight changed throughout the day. His style was inspirational to Impressionist artists (see room 87), who would come later. This painting of an old war ship and a steam tugboat symbolized how the world was becoming more modern. The setting sun is a symbol for the old ways of the world coming to an end.

ZOOM IN

ROMANTICISM
Emotional Art

ROOM 76

Romanticism was about showing emotion in art. Artists made passionate history paintings showing people filled with fear, bravery, love, and sadness. They also painted enormous, inspiring landscapes. They didn't worry so much about hiding their brushstrokes, like Neo-Classical artists (see room 74). All of the colors and visible brushstrokes in their work were seen as proof of the artists' strong emotions!

LOST AT SEA

THÉODORE GÉRICAULT, THE RAFT OF THE MEDUSA, 1819

When a ship called the Medusa wrecked on a sandbank off the coast of Africa in 1816, there weren't enough lifeboats for everyone, so those left behind built a raft on which to sail for help. Over thirteen days, 150 men on the small raft fought to stay alive until they were saved. Most fell overboard or starved; only 10 survived. This huge, life-size painting shows the moment the men spotted a ship in the distance. An African crew member named Jean Charles frantically waves his shirt at the tiny speck, hoping for rescue. See if you can spot the feelings of excitement, desperation, and hopelessness on the faces of the crew.

ART DETECTIVE

In literature, Romanticism inspired stories such as *Grimm's Fairy Tales*, published in 1812. These include the famous tales of *Hansel and Gretel*, *Cinderella*, and more.

EUROPEAN REALISM
Paintings for All

ROOM 77

Rules—the art academies loved them! But over time, artists became frustrated by the strict ideas about painting historical and mythological subjects. So in the 1800s, the European Realist movement grew. Artists wanted to paint scenes that were truer to life than stories of goddesses and kings. They painted people hard at work and showed the difficulties of the poor in order to reveal the lives of all people.

PAINTING REAL LIFE

GUSTAVE COURBET, THE ARTIST'S STUDIO, 1854–55

Gustave Courbet believed in painting things he could see, not scenes from myths. This made portraits of working-class lives just as important as history paintings or portraits of the upper class. In this huge painting, Courbet is painting at his studio. To the left are portraits of peasants and workers, and to the right are images of his friends. He wrote that the painting shows "the whole world coming to me to be painted."

IN THE COUNTRYSIDE

ROSA BONHEUR, HAYMAKING, AUVERGNE, 1855

This scene of rural life won a gold medal during the 1855 World's Fair in Paris. The painter, Rosa Bonheur, was as brave as she was talented. She didn't care what anyone thought about her living with her girlfriend or wearing "men's" clothing. She said one reason she liked to wear trousers was because it was easier to paint in them when she was working with animal subjects.

European Painting 1600–1850

GALLERY O
Pacific Art

The South Pacific region is made up of thousands of islands. They are split into smaller island groups called Melanesia, Polynesia, and Micronesia. This gallery will show their unique works, from giant stone statues to smaller spiritual artworks.

Long ago, when sea levels were much lower, people sailed or paddled to the Pacific Islands from Southeast Asia. They moved between the islands, making them their home. Their stories and artistic techniques were passed on through spoken word and by example from person to person.

Native Pacific Islanders spoke (and still speak) many languages and have unique cultures and artistic styles. Some objects were made from stone and wood, so some of them are still around today. Others, such as objects made from delicate spider webs or flowers, have disappeared. Think of it like building a giant snowman. It's still special, even if it melts away! This is one reason why the art shown from this region does not go back as far in time as some other galleries on display.

The art from across this region includes images of gods, spirits, and ancestors from the people who lived there. Step into the gallery to see how these artworks helped connect humans to the spiritual world.

ROOMS 78–79

142 The Ultimate Art Museum

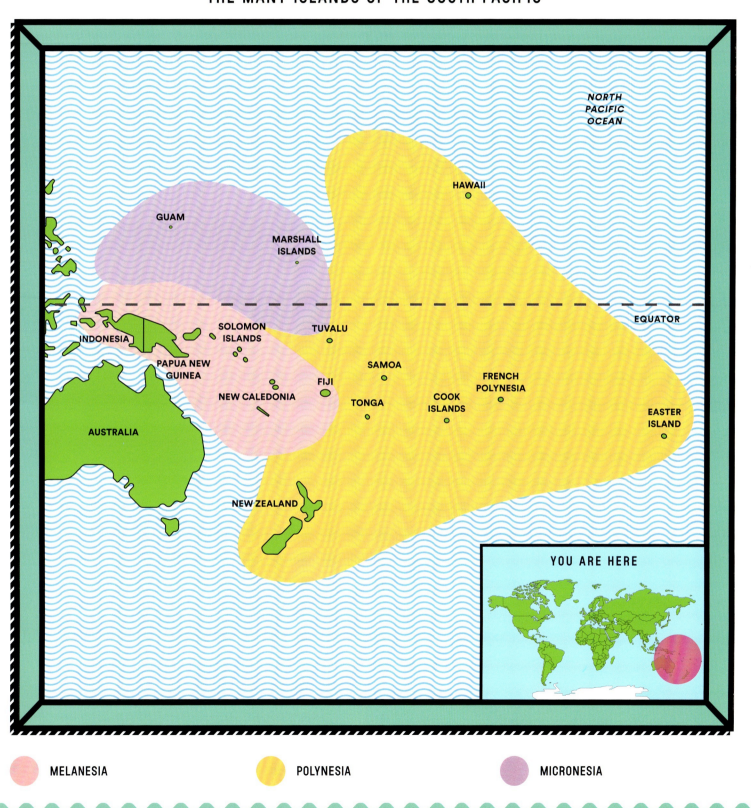

POLYNESIA AND MICRONESIA
A Sea of Islands

ROOM 78

If you drew a circle on a map around Polynesia and Micronesia, it would contain more islands than you could count! These include Hawaii, New Zealand, and even an island named Christmas. Many native cultures across these islands believe in *mana*, which is a supernatural power that can be found in important people, like warriors or leaders or in objects, such as some sculptures. *Mana* is protected by spiritual rules called *tapu*.

SACRED ANCESTORS
MOAI FIGURES, c.1100–1650

These large stone figures, called *moai*, from the island of Rapa Nui (Easter Island), are carved from hardened volcanic ash. They were placed on top of sacred platforms, called *ahu*, to honor living chiefs, ancestors, or clans. The native people of the island believed the sculptures could help pass *mana* from ancestors to current leaders. The heads were made big because this is believed to be the part of the body with the most *mana*. The eyes originally had shells or stones placed inside, and some statues had painted designs.

A SPIRITUAL DOORWAY
DOOR LINTEL, LATE 1840s

A lintel is the horizontal section you pass under every time you go through a door. Throughout Polynesia and Micronesia, specially carved lintels were made for the doorways of sacred spaces. These lintels have *tapu* because they define a sacred space. When a person walks under it, the lintel shows that they have crossed between the sacred spaces of different gods, or from a nonreligious space to a religious one. This lintel shows Tane, the god of the forest in the Maori culture, and his brothers, pushing the Earth and sky apart.

ZOOM IN

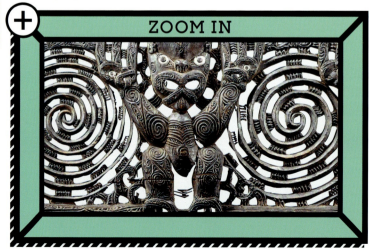

144 The Ultimate Art Museum

MELANESIA
Carving Connections

ROOM 79

Over 1,000 languages are spoken on the islands of Melanesia, and the art styles and materials the people use are just as diverse. Even the human body becomes an artwork through paint or tattoos. Across Melanesia, masks and carvings helped people connect with their ancestors. They used them in dances and rituals to honor loved ones, show respect to the spirit world, and as part of funeral celebrations.

A MASKED DANCE
ROM MASK, 1800

The island of Ambrym is a volcano, complete with lakes of lava! The people there have a secret group, the members of which wear a rom mask during sacred ceremonies. The rom are believed to give a home to ancestor spirits temporarily, while they are being used. The long "hair" made of coconut fiber overlaps a thick fiber costume that covers the wearer's body during dances. Watching groups of these dancers must be a powerful sight!

DECORATIVE PROTECTION
WARRIOR SHIELD, FIRST HALF OF THE 1800s

This shield comes from the Solomon Islands to the northeast of Australia. Shields like this could be used during battles and ceremonies. This shield was made with a basket weaving technique. Both the color and the white shells were added after. The intricate pattern makes a human shape in the black-and-red design. As it is so delicate, it's likely this shield was only used for rituals, not war.

Pacific Art 145

GALLERY P
Arts of Africa 1300-1900

The African continent is huge! Within this big space there are many unique kingdoms, communities, and artistic styles. The traditional arts of Africa celebrate leaders and tell the stories of Africa's great empires and civilizations.

Over thousands of years, cultures across Africa have used different woods, metals, ivory, cloth, and clay to create art with spiritual and practical purposes. Objects may be religious, share stories about people's families, or show portraits of important people, such as kings. Many works are figurative—that means they show people or animals—while others use abstract shapes and patterns that have been passed down within communities over generations.

To help explore the art of this vast continent, this gallery will look at objects by geographical areas. Try to see what different subjects, influences, and materials you notice across the different rooms. And don't forget you can also see another style of African art in the ancient Egyptian gallery (see gallery C)!

Come, let's travel far and wide to explore the exciting creativity and diversity of the art of the African continent.

ROOMS 80–84

146 The Ultimate Art Museum

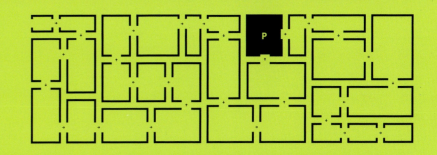

REGIONS OF THE AFRICAN CONTINENT

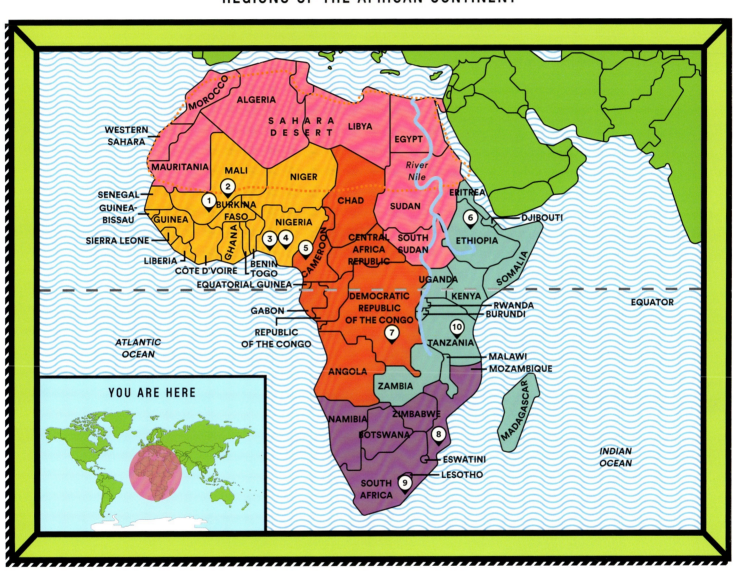

Arts of Africa 1300–1900 147

WEST AFRICA
Showing Respect

ROOM 80

West Africa has been home to large kingdoms and cultures, many of which still exist today! These include the Yoruba culture and the Benin people, who carved sculptures from bronze and wood to celebrate important figures. The Dogon culture made sculptures of gods to protect certain groups of people, such as hunters. Artworks across West Africa celebrate all kinds of powerful leaders, from kings to mothers.

A YORUBA KING
ONI, 1300s–EARLY 1400s

HONOR YOUR MOTHER
PENDANT MASK, 1500s

Oni is the word for "king" in the Yoruba language. This small bronze statue shows the beaded details of a king's royal costume. The sculpture is thought to come from the ancient city of Ife in southwest Nigeria, where many bronze pieces like this were made. In Yoruba culture, Ife is believed to be the place where the gods sculpted the first living humans from clay. Do you notice how lifelike the figure's face is? This is a clue that this is a portrait of a particular king.

The Benin kingdom is known for how well it made bronze sculptures. But artists were also skilled in using other materials, like the ivory work you can see here. This ivory mask was probably made to honor *Iyoba* Idia, the Queen Mother. *Iyoba* is the title for the queen mother in Edo, the language of the Benin kingdom. The *oba* ("king" in Edo) would have worn this to honor her during special yearly ceremonies and rituals.

PERFECT BALANCE
SEATED COUPLE, 1500s–1800s

CEREMONIAL STATUES
GWANDUSU, 1400s–1900s

This sculpture from Mali is an example of balance and symmetry. Can you see the similarities in each of the figures? On the back of this sculpture, the woman (left) has a baby on her back, and the man (right) has a carrier for his arrows. Neither side is bigger than the other. They are different, but balanced, just like the roles for men and women in their community. Sculptures like this may have been displayed during funerals of important men from the Dogon culture (in Mali and Burkina Faso).

A *Gwandusu* is a powerful figure. In the Bamana culture of Mali, she is believed to help women have children. This is why she is shown holding a baby. She is also a symbol of beauty and good character. And she's tough! Even though Bamana women traditionally didn't go hunting, these figures are often shown with a knife and hat worn by the hunters. *Gwandusu* were put on display during ceremonies for a special Bamana society called Jo.

CENTRAL AFRICA
Important Portraits

Art is serious business! In some parts of Central Africa, traditional objects were used to reach agreements, record history, or show a person's power. Art across this area includes wooden sculptures and elaborate masks that were decorated with leaves, beads, and cowrie shells. These small shells were a sign that a person was rich and important. At one time, they were even used as money in parts of Africa and Asia.

A ROYAL DOUBLE
N'DOP, KING NYIM MISHÉ MISHYÁÁNG MÁMBÚL, 1700s

Have you ever wished you could be in more than one place at once? In the Kuba kingdom, the king had his very own royal solution to this problem! An *n'dop* was a carved sculpture of the king that could represent him when he could not be somewhere. Each royal sculpture like this has an *ibol* placed in front of it. The *ibol* is an object that is the symbol for a king. The drum here is the symbol for King Nyim Mishé miShyááng máMbúl. This sculpture is the oldest known example of an *n'dop*.

DECORATIONS OF POWER
ROYAL MASK, BEFORE 1880

A lot of information can be discovered from a mask. This one from the Bamum people has precious beads, shells, and brass and shows that the owner came from a wealthy background. The red, spider-like design on the crown is a symbol of wisdom. The large ears, eyes, and open mouth tell us it is linked to royalty. Masks like these were worn by members of the powerful *kwifoyn* societies. Members would wear the mask and do a slow dance at important events, such as funerals or harvest festivals.

ETHIOPIAN CHRISTIAN ART
Trade, Art, and Beliefs

ROOM 82

Let's go back to the Aksumite empire (c.80 BCE–940 CE) in present-day Ethiopia and Eritrea. The empire existed along important trade routes where people traveled and shared ideas. This included the Byzantines (see gallery F), who were Christian. Around the year 330 CE, King Azana converted his kingdom to Christianity. From then on, artists in Ethiopia made stunning paintings, crosses, and other forms of Christian art.

SPREAD THE WORD
PROCESSIONAL CROSS, 1400s

PAINTING THE LIFE OF JESUS
THE ASCENSION, ILLUMINATED GOSPEL, 1300s–1400s

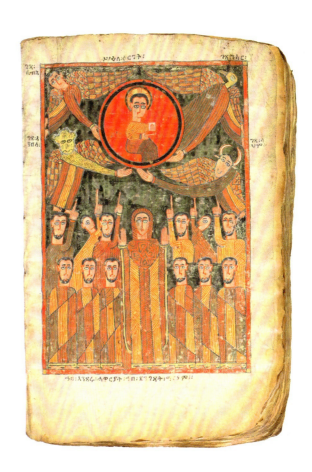

Processional crosses were made to be carried during religious ceremonies. This style of copper cross has a design common in the Ethiopian town of Lalibela. The city is famous for its large churches carved completely out of rock! This cross would have been placed on a pole and carried by religious leaders as worshippers followed.

This is a page from an illuminated manuscript of the Amhara people from Ethiopia. The book included twenty colorful paintings of scenes from the Bible on vellum. Vellum pages are made from animal skins. Historians believe the illustrations in this book were done by two artists working in a monastery. The bold colors and style of drawing were inspired by earlier Byzantine designs (see p.50). This scene shows the moment Jesus rose up to heaven.

👁 Can you find four other illustrated book pages in this wing?

Arts of Africa 1300–1900 151

SOUTHERN AFRICA
Uniquely Useful Art

ROOM 83

Cultures in southern Africa, such as those of the Nguni and Tsonga people, used natural materials, such as wood and clay, to make objects with a practical use. Clay could be molded into pottery and wood could be carved into headrests or other furniture. But just because something is practical, doesn't mean it can't look interesting! Objects could be shaped like animals or covered in creative patterns and textures.

A SPIKY BULL

LONGHORN BULL SNUFF CONTAINER, LATE 1800s

Beware of the spiky texture when picking up this little snuff (powdered tobacco) container! This design is a style used by the Nguni people from South Africa. To make the shape, the artist pressed a mixture of clay, blood, and scraps of animal skin into a mold. After it was removed, the rough details of the bull's fur were added by hand. The hole in the top originally had a stopper.

👁 Can you find another bull container in wing one?

A PROTECTIVE PILLOW

TSONGA HEADREST, 1800s–1900s

Headrests have been made across Africa for thousands of years. They were made to hold the head at the neck or jawline while sleeping, like a pillow. A headrest's shape could also help protect complicated hairstyles, and was believed to connect people to the spiritual world while they dreamed. Headrests from the Tsonga people are called *mhamba*, which describes an object that connects a person to the gods.

? ART DETECTIVE

In the Blombos Cave in South Africa an entire paint workshop was unearthed. Archaeologists think it is around 100,000 years old! This could be the earliest recorded art, from the time of the very first humans that lived in Africa.

EAST AFRICA AND MADAGASCAR
Community Leaders

ROOM 84

The countries of East Africa stretch up the coast of the Indian Ocean and out into an area known as the Horn of Africa. That's the part that looks a little like a rhinoceros's horn! Madagascar is an island country off the eastern coast. The art from these areas include colorful beaded objects and figurative carvings made to honor important occasions, such as ceremonies for moving from childhood to adulthood.

FOR ALL TO SEE
SAKALAVA HAZOMANGA, 1600s–LATE 1700s

THE CHIEF'S CHAIR
HEHE THRONE, LATE 1800s

This wooden sculpture shows a couple from the Sakalava ethnic group in Madagascar. The man and woman both stand in the same pose to show their connection to each other. It was carved to go on top of a tall pole called a *hazomanga*. These poles were placed outside of the homes of community elders. The poles were up to 6 feet tall and placed in an area for all to see. *Hazomanga* were also places where people could pray and perform ceremonies.

This magnificent example of a throne was made by the Hehe people of Tanzania. The high-backed chair has female features that make the sitter appear to be sitting on her lap! Chairs with high backs were usually used by a chief. The head shows carved details of scarification, which is when designs are created on the skin through small cuts. A hollow tube under the seat may have been used to raise the throne high for special occasions.

Arts of Africa 1300–1900

A WALK IN THE GARDEN

Want some fresh air? Take a stroll in our garden. Our artists have planted some wild surprises unlike any others for you.

AN EYE-POPPING POPPY!

GEORGIA O'KEEFFE, RED POPPY, NO. VI, 1928

Lean in close and enjoy the view! Georgia O'Keeffe's paintings zoom in so much that the flowers look like abstract designs. Her paintings help people see their shapes and colors in new ways.

PAINTING FOR SCIENCE

MARIA SIBYLLA MERIAN, CITRUS AURANTIUM WITH ROTHSCHILDIA AUROTA MOTH, 1705

There are some interesting insects hidden among the garden leaves. Maria Sibylla Merian was a naturalist and illustrator who watched insects closely and drew detailed pictures of them.

A STARTLING STORM

HENRI ROUSSEAU, TIGER IN A TROPICAL STORM (SURPRISED), 1891

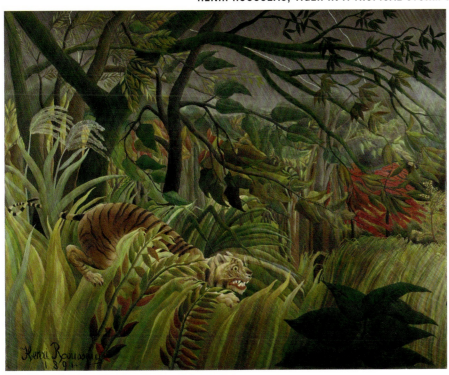

Watch out for the tiger! Henri Rousseau painted this tiger crouching among thick jungle leaves. Its eyes are wide, and it looks like it was given a shock by the lighting flashing in the background.

MAKING PATTERNS WITH FLOWERS

GUSTAV KLIMT, FLOWER GARDEN, 1905-07

You've seen one poppy up close—now it's time to step back and take in a whole flower patch! In many of Gustav Klimt's paintings, he shows tiny colorful shapes that come together to show a larger bright picture, like the flowers of a garden.

WING 3

MODERN AND CONTEMPORARY ART

ALMOST ANYTHING IS POSSIBLE IN ART!

It's an exciting time and you're living in it right now...

This wing displays artworks from the era of making "art for art's sake." This means making art that does not have a set purpose, like teaching a religious lesson or celebrating the dead. In this wing, artists created works that were experimental and personal. They used unusual materials and tried exciting techniques.

INSIDE THIS WING YOU WILL DISCOVER...

- Abstract Art
- Rebels
- Activists
- Dreamscapes
- Photography
- Floating Worlds
- Glowing Lights
- Collage
- Splattering
- Art Outdoors
- Trash to Treasure
- Pictures That Pop
- Moving Pictures

GALLERY Q
Modern Art

It's time for an art revolution! Prepare to question everything, from what makes something "art" to why it should be made and what it can look like.

For hundreds of years, artists in Europe and North America were focused on making art that looked lifelike. It was a sign of real talent if you could paint or sculpt an apple that looked like an apple. In this gallery, artists focus on different subjects and find new inspirations for making art. Some artists make artworks that don't show anything recognizable at all, while others show familiar objects in new styles. What a scandal these first modern artists caused!

The invention of photography in the 1820s caused another big change in art. As photography became more popular and easier to do, artists didn't need to paint lifelike pictures anymore. Painters began to use wild colors and unusual shapes. European artists began looking further afield, finding inspiration in artworks such as African masks or Japanese prints. Now, two people might paint the same object but each painting could look totally different!

ROOMS 85–106

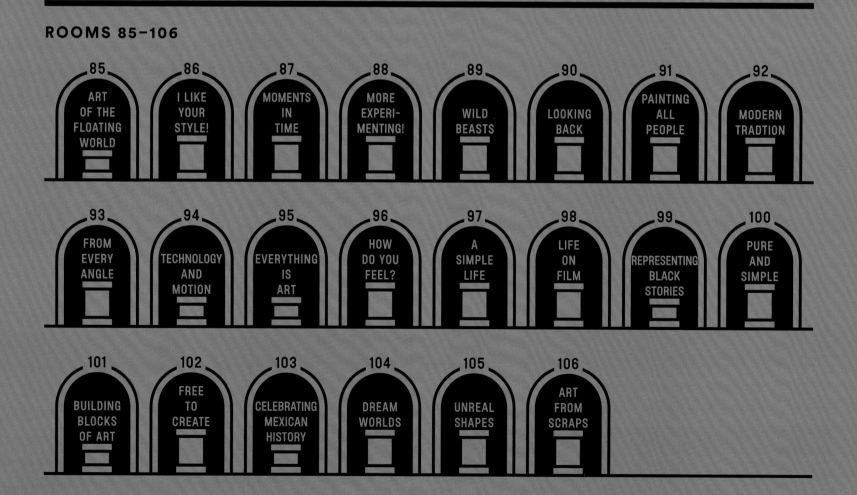

85 ART OF THE FLOATING WORLD
86 I LIKE YOUR STYLE!
87 MOMENTS IN TIME
88 MORE EXPERIMENTING!
89 WILD BEASTS
90 LOOKING BACK
91 PAINTING ALL PEOPLE
92 MODERN TRADTION
93 FROM EVERY ANGLE
94 TECHNOLOGY AND MOTION
95 EVERYTHING IS ART
96 HOW DO YOU FEEL?
97 A SIMPLE LIFE
98 LIFE ON FILM
99 REPRESENTING BLACK STORIES
100 PURE AND SIMPLE
101 BUILDING BLOCKS OF ART
102 FREE TO CREATE
103 CELEBRATING MEXICAN HISTORY
104 DREAM WORLDS
105 UNREAL SHAPES
106 ART FROM SCRAPS

158 The Ultimate Art Museum

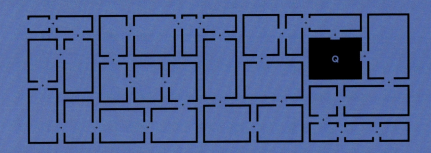

MODERN ART: STYLES THAT SWEPT THROUGH THE WORLD (AND WHERE THEY BEGAN)

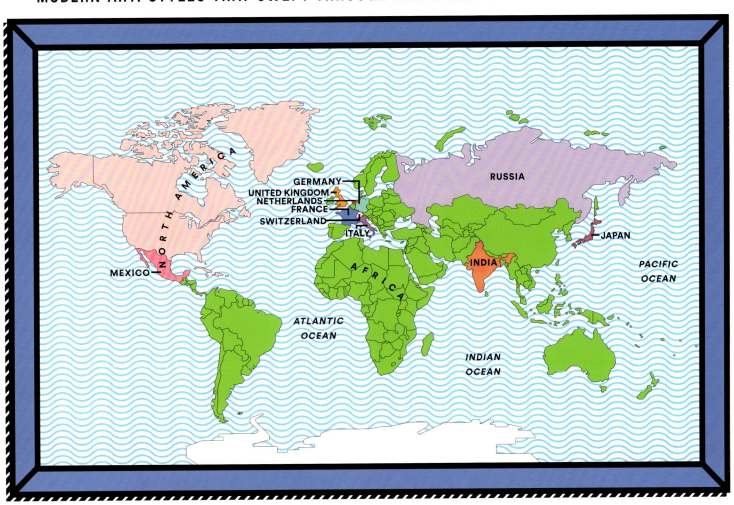

AS ARTISTS TRAVELED AROUND THE WORLD, THEY TOOK THEIR GREAT IDEAS WITH THEM! THIS MAP SHOWS WERE SOME OF THE MOVEMENTS IN THIS GALLERY FIRST BEGAN.

- IMPRESSIONISM
- CUBISM
- SURREALISM
- PRE-RAPHAELITES
- AMERICAN REALISM
- AMERICAN REGIONALISM
- FUTURISM
- DADA
- EXPRESSIONISM
- SUPREMATISM
- DE STIJL
- THE BENGAL SCHOOL
- MEXICAN MURALISM
- *UKIYO-E*

Modern Art 159

UKIYO-E
Art of the Floating World

ROOM 85

The Japanese word *ukiyo-e* means "pictures of the floating world." These woodblock prints and paintings showed the bustling and exciting entertainment areas in Japan's big cities, particularly Tokyo. Pictures could show famous actors, sumo wrestlers, and more. *Ukiyo-e* started out in the 1600s, and by the 1800s, artists of the floating world were also making prints that highlighted the beauty of Japanese landscapes.

RIDE THE WAVE

KATSUSHIKA HOKUSAI, THE GREAT WAVE OF KANAGAWA, c.1830–32

In this famous Japanese *ukiyo-e* image, a giant wave is crashing down on three boats full of fishermen. The white crests of the waves look like claws ready to pull the crews under. It's all so exciting, but this picture is actually about the sacred volcano, Mount Fuji, in the background. It is part of Katsushika Hokusai's woodblock print series called Thirty-six Views of Mt Fuji. He decided to print landscapes instead of the city and changed what *ukiyo-e* artworks could show.

ART DETECTIVE

To make these prints, **artisans** carved a picture designed by the artist onto a woodblock. The picture was then transferred onto paper. Because each color needed a different woodblock, artisans sometimes carved up to 20 different blocks to make one picture!

JAPANESE INSPIRATION IN EUROPE
I Like Your Style!

ROOM 86

In 1867, there was an international art fair in Paris, where people shared new inventions, art, and cultural objects. This was the first time Japan had taken part, and it caused a sensation. People were amazed—they had never seen this style of art before. A craze in Europe for Japanese fashion and art soon took hold. When European artists saw these artworks, it influenced the way they painted patterns, shadows, and shapes.

WOOD-BLOCK WONDERS

UTAGAWA HIROSHIGE, BAMBOO YARDS, KYŌBASHI BRIDGE, c.1857–58

This colorful woodblock print comes from a series titled One Hundred Famous Views of Edo. It shows popular tourist sites in Edo (known as Tokyo today). The tall, gray poles in the background are bamboo stalks—important building materials in Japan. Can you spot the third man from the left on the bridge? The woodblock carver hid his signature on the man's lantern!

BUILDING BRIDGES

JAMES MCNEILL WHISTLER, NOCTURNE: BLUE AND GOLD– OLD BATTERSEA BRIDGE, c.1872–75

The American artist James McNeill Whistler is one of the many artists inspired by Hiroshige. Can you spot how the arch and position of this bridge is similar to the bridge in Hiroshige's print? The background also shows golden flecks that are similar to another Hiroshige print that shows fireworks bursting across the sky. Whistler painted this as part of a series showing London's River Thames at night.

Modern Art 161

IMPRESSIONISM
Moments in Time

ROOM 87

The Impressionists were the rebels of French art! They didn't want to paint in the same styles that were usually displayed at the famous Salon exhibition in Paris, so they created their own. Impressionist paintings can be easy to spot—they liked to paint an "impression" of how something looked in a moment of time, with quick and visible brushstrokes.

FUN AND GAMES
BERTHE MORISOT, HIDE AND SEEK, 1873

Berthe Morisot was a French painter and a very important member of the Impressionists. At the start, she was the only woman in this group of painters. Morisot showed her work at every Impressionist exhibition except one, and even helped organize and pay for their first exhibition. She had met some members of the group, such as Monet, while copying paintings at the Louvre art museum in Paris. This was one way that many artists improved their skills at that time. She also enjoyed painting scenes outdoors, called *plein air* painting. Morisot is known for quick, fat brushstrokes that look like sketches. Many of her paintings show private moments from the lives of upper-class women at home and with their children. This painting shows a woman and her daughter playing a game of hide and seek.

👁 For other pictures of mothers and children, go to pp. 91, 121, 131, 163, 175, 217.

MAKE AN IMPRESSION
CLAUDE MONET, IMPRESSION, SUNRISE, 1872

This painting by Claude Monet gave the Impressionists their name! This group liked painting outside, so they could see how light changed throughout the day. Here, Monet painted the sun rising over the port in his hometown of Le Havre. Sometimes sunlight is bright and yellow, or sometimes it is warm and orange as it is here. The changing colors of light throughout the day can give very different impressions of the same subject.

➕ ZOOM IN

162 The Ultimate Art Museum

A NIGHT OUT
ÉDOUARD MANET, A BAR AT THE FOLIES-BERGÈRE, 1881–82

Édouard Manet's work links two different styles: Impressionism and Realism. Although he started working in a European Realist style (see p.141), his loose brushstrokes and rebellious attitude hugely influenced the Impressionists. This painting shows a woman working at a popular music hall. The mirror behind her reflects the people there. Can you spot the way in which Manet uses loose strokes to paint an impression of a busy crowd? The man to the right is possibly a self-portrait.

👁 For other clever ways artists have used mirrors in art go to pp.122, 130, 200, 204!

DANCING IN AIR
EDGAR DEGAS, MADEMOISELLE LA LA AT THE CIRQUE FERNANDO, 1879

Edgar Degas was part of the Impressionist group but also thought of himself as a Realist painter (see p.141) because he loved to paint everyday life. Degas loved painting small moments from entertaining events, such as the ballet and horse races. He often painted these from unusual angles, which was not easy to do. This painting looks upward at the circus acrobat known as Mademoiselle La La as she clenches a rope in her teeth to swing from the ceiling.

ROCKING THE BOAT
MARY CASSATT, THE BOATING PARTY, 1894

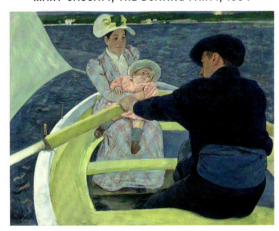

Mary Cassatt was an American painter who lived and worked in France for much of her life. Do you notice that there is not much shading on the figures and boat in this scene? This is because Cassatt was inspired by Japanese *ukiyo-e* prints (see p.160), which showed fewer shadows. This effect makes three-dimensional objects appear flat.

Modern Art 163

POST-IMPRESSIONISM
More Experimenting!

Because *post* means "after," Post-Impressionism came after Impressionism and includes a mixture of styles. These artists learned how the Impressionists used light and color, but they wanted to do more than just capture a moment in time. Post-Impressionists experimented with wild colors, new techniques, new subject matters, and different materials—they took modern art to another level!

PAINTING WITH POINTS

GEORGES SEURAT, A SUNDAY AFTERNOON ON THE ISLAND OF LA GRANDE JATTE, 1884–86

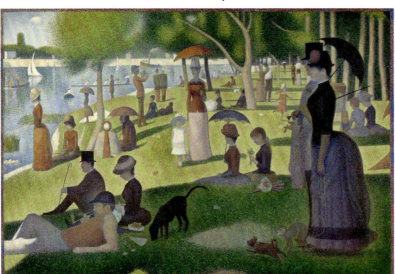

This nearly life-size painting shows Parisian families having fun on a Sunday afternoon. Look closely. Can you see that it's made from thousands of tiny dots? Seurat used little points of color to build up a whole picture. This technique is called **pointillism**.

ZOOM IN

SWIRLS IN THE SKY

VINCENT VAN GOGH, STARRY NIGHT, 1889

Try not to get dizzy as you take in this painting of a quiet town under a starry sky. Vincent van Gogh is famous for artworks such as this, which show layers of thick paint and strong, visible brushstrokes. The technique of using thick layers of paint is called **impasto**. Van Gogh created around 2,100 artworks in his lifetime but didn't become famous until after he died. He was born in the Netherlands and only decided to become a painter at age 27. He traveled across Europe, making friends with other artists and painting the places he visited. Toward the end of his life, he felt unwell and struggled with mental-health problems. He painted this view from the window of a hospital during his stay there.

164 The Ultimate Art Museum

FAUVISM
Wild Beasts

ROOM 89

Watch out for these wild beasts! The Fauvists got their name after an art exhibition in 1905. A French art critic saw the bold colors in their work and said it looked like *fauves* (wild beasts) had been painting!

Instead of using realistic shading, the Fauvists purposefully used unnatural colors and bigger brushstrokes. They placed bright colors next to each other to show **contrast** and make them stand out.

FLAT BUT FULL

HENRI MATISSE, RED ROOM (HARMONY IN RED), 1908

Henri Matisse was the most famous "beast." He believed that flat canvases shouldn't look three-dimensional. Can you tell where the tablecloth ends, and the wallpaper begins? Is the landscape a painting or a window? Matisse doesn't show shadows or bright lights, so the blocks of color look flat and can fool the eye.

Modern Art 165

PRE-RAPHAELITES
Looking Back

ROOM 90

For a long time, English academies taught art styles inspired by Renaissance artists such as Raphael (see p.120). In 1848, a group of artists decided they preferred the details and colors of the Quattrocento (see room 65) artists before ("pre") Raphael. They became known as the Pre-Raphaelites. Their paintings show every detail, such as tiny leaves or people's faces. They believed this was the truest way to show the world.

STRENGTH AND NATURE
EVELYN DE MORGAN, FLORA, 1894

In this painting, you can see how Pre-Raphaelites, such as Evelyn De Morgan, were inspired by Quattrocento artists. This painting shows Flora, the Roman goddess of flowers, whom Botticelli painted in a piece called *Primavera*. Flick back to p.118 in wing two. Can you see how De Morgan was inspired by the rippling, flowery dress and detailed greenery in Botticelli's painting? De Morgan was skilled at painting people draped in heavy fabrics. Her work often features strong women because she was a firm believer in promoting equal rights for women.

FLOATING AMONG FLOWERS
JOHN EVERETT MILLAIS, OPHELIA, 1851

Everywhere you look in this painting, there are crisp details to discover. John Everett Millais thought like a scientist so he wanted the painting to be as true to life as possible. To see the details of what a clothed woman looked like in water, he asked the artist Elizabeth Siddal to model in a bathtub. She ended up catching a cold and Millais had to pay her doctor's bills!

AMERICAN REALISM
Painting All People

ROOM 91

American realist paintings reflect the lives of all people, especially workers and the poor. The paintings show the story of a growing and changing United States, including small towns and bustling cities. Artists offered a glimpse inside shops, street corners, and homes. Some artists showed the loneliness that could be felt in big cities. Others captured activities of everyday life that hadn't been shown in paintings before.

A QUIET DINNER

EDWARD HOPPER, NIGHTHAWKS, 1942

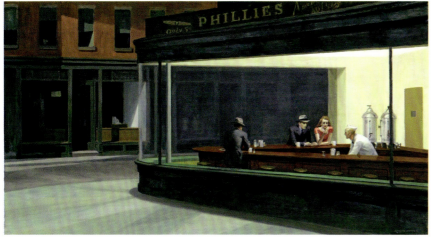

This calm scene shows people in an all-night diner after the other shops on the street have closed. Even though we can see into the giant window, there is no door in sight! This makes a viewer feel very distant and left out. Many of Hopper's paintings show people in similar quiet American settings, such as modern homes or offices.

BOXING SHOWS

GEORGE BELLOWS, CLUB NIGHT, 1907

George Bellows's paintings show the exciting action of big American cities. Boxing matches were illegal in New York when this painting was made. People got around the rules by creating "clubs" that allowed boxing.

ART AND TRUTH

HENRY OSSAWA TANNER, THE BANJO LESSON, 1893

Henry Ossawa Tanner's paintings were influenced by his art training in the United States and Paris, as well as his experiences as a Black American man. Slavery in the US had ended less than 30 years before this work was painted. At this time, Black people in America were often shown as stereotypes, especially as minstrels (entertainers). Stereotypes are unfair descriptions that group people together. Tanner wanted to break minstrel stereotypes by showing a Black musician in a more personal way. He shows an older man playing a banjo to teach a child and not as an entertainer.

ZOOM IN

ROOM 92

AFRICAN MASKS
Modern Tradition

People across the African continent have been making masks for thousands of years. Masks can be worn as part of a costume during rituals and ceremonies. Different cultures in Africa have their own traditional styles of masks, but they often use abstract shapes and patterns and interesting materials to create faces. Many artists, including Picasso and Matisse, were hugely inspired by their designs and structure.

WHAT'S IN A MASK?
NGAADY-A-MWAASH MASK, LATE 1800s–EARLY 1900s

You can read parts of this mask like a story. The beads going down the nose and mouth show that this is a pure and important figure. The lines from her eyes are tears. The mask is of Ngaady-A-Mwaash, a legendary wife of the first Kuba King who founded the kingdom (part of the Democratic Republic of Congo). In performances, she appears alongside two male masks that represent ancestors who competed for her love.

PATH OF THE ANCESTORS
LURUYA MASK, 1800s–1900s

This tall mask was made by the Bwa people of Burkina Faso. Masks like these are made to honor an ancient ancestor named Luruya, an excellent but small hunter. Can you see the lines on the circular face and the rectangle above them? These are the "path of the ancestors," a reminder about following the rules. These are similar to the scar lines the Bwa people wear on their faces.

168 The Ultimate Art Museum

CUBISM
From Every Angle

ROOM 93

How can you show multiple sides of something at the same time? First, Paul Cézanne (see p.96) explored this idea, then Pablo Picasso and Georges Braque asked themselves the same question. And so began the Cubist movement! It was a style that chopped and rearranged images. Cubists blended inspirations from African arts and ancient European cultures into their work. Eventually, Cubism found its way into other art styles too.

MUSICAL PIECES

GEORGES BRAQUE, VIOLIN AND PITCHER, 1909–10

Do you see the violin? Different parts appear at the same time, including its top and sides. This is because Georges Braque has broken up the object and put them back together at impossible angles. Works like this are part of the **Analytical Cubist** style. Braque analyzed the object in detail and experimented with how to show its entire three-dimensional shape on a flat surface.

INSPIRED BY AFRICAN ART

PABLO PICASSO, HEAD OF A SLEEPING WOMAN, 1907

Pablo Picasso's artwork can be split into periods of time. These periods are inspired by different styles, such as Analytical Cubism, or are defined by colors, such as his Blue Period. He was always experimenting to find new ways to show the world! Picasso created this portrait at a time when he was greatly inspired by African masks and sculptures he had admired in museums. He took ideas from those traditional objects to develop his early Cubist style.

Modern Art 169

FUTURISM
Technology and Motion

Out with the old and in with the new! Futurist artists thought museums focused on the past too much. In the early 1900s, the world around them was changing in such an incredible way. Cars were zooming down streets and planes were flying across the sky. Why not celebrate this in art? Futurists borrowed some of their style from the Cubists but focused on movement and celebrating new technology.

EVERY STEP OF THE WAY

MARCEL DUCHAMP, NUDE DESCENDING A STAIRCASE (NO. 2), 1912

Marcel Duchamp was inspired by the work of early photographers. He liked how photos could show many actions at once, like slowly moving down the stairs. Duchamp wanted to try this in his painting. Here the same figure is repeated, with the lines swooping to show movement. Duchamp submitted the painting to a Cubist exhibition, but they rejected it because they thought that experimenting with movement was too Futurist.

ON THE RUN

UMBERTO BOCCIONI, UNIQUE FORMS OF CONTINUITY IN SPACE, 1913

What if you could make a statue look like it was moving? Umberto Boccioni tried to do just that with this bronze sculpture. The humanlike figure seems to be pushing forward, against a strong force. Boccioni created this feeling by building areas that stick out backward, as if the figure is being whipped by wind as it moves. The power and movement of this work is similar to the modern machines that the Futurists admired.

DADA
Everything is Art

ROOM 95

This art movement is nonsense. No, really! The Dada movement embraced the absurd by experimenting, breaking all the rules, and challenging what can be thought of as art. Some artists took ordinary items that were lying around and called them "readymade" sculptures. Dada art was a reaction to the horrors of the First World War, and what better gift to bring lightness to the world than through embracing the absurd?

MAKING A SPLASH
MARCEL DUCHAMP (ATTRIBUTED TO), FOUNTAIN, 1964 (REPLICA OF 1917 ORIGINAL)

A SHREDDING IRON
MAN RAY, THE GIFT, 1972 (EDITIONED REPLICA AFTER 1921 ORIGINAL)

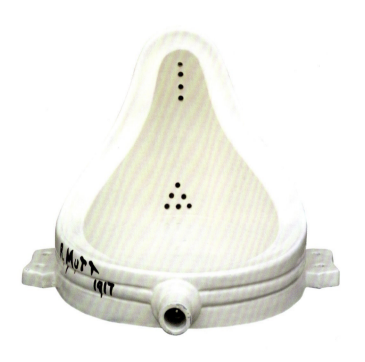

This readymade sculpture of a urinal by the French artist Marcel Duchamp was mysteriously submitted to an exhibition under the name "R. Mutt." The exhibition was meant to accept all entries, but this piece was rejected when the directors declared that a toilet could not be art! Duchamp was very upset about the decision. He said that the sculpture belonged in a gallery because the artist "chose" it and gave it a new name. This made it art.

It wouldn't be a good idea to do your ironing with this readymade sculpture by Man Ray. The artist made the iron unusable by gluing on a row of brass tacks! This mixture of opposites is a classically Dada thing to do because it has created a nonsense, useless object. Ray meant for his friends to have a chance to win this piece at his first exhibition, which is why it's called *The Gift*. Sadly, it was stolen before he could give it away.

EXPRESSIONISM
How Do You Feel?

ROOM 96

Do you ever get really filled up with emotions? Expressionism was a movement of artists that showed emotions through painting. Artists used bright colors, distorted shapes, and visible brushstrokes that matched the energy of their feelings. The early styles began with artists such as Vincent Van Gogh (see p.164), and was later developed by German artists. German Expressionism is split into Die Brücke and Der Blaue Reiter.

EARLY EXPRESSIONISM
EDVARD MUNCH, THE SCREAM, 1893

When the Norwegian painter Edvard Munch went walking with two friends at sunset, he observed how the sky can turn into shocking shades of red and orange. Munch thought that it looked as if nature itself was screaming! He painted this feeling, with his two friends carrying on as normal in front of him. This painting, with its full and raw emotion, is said to have inspired the Expressionist movement in the neighboring country of Germany.

👁 How the colors in this sunset compare to Monet's sunrise on p.162?

BUILDING A BRIDGE
ERNST LUDWIG KIRCHNER, STREET, BERLIN, 1913

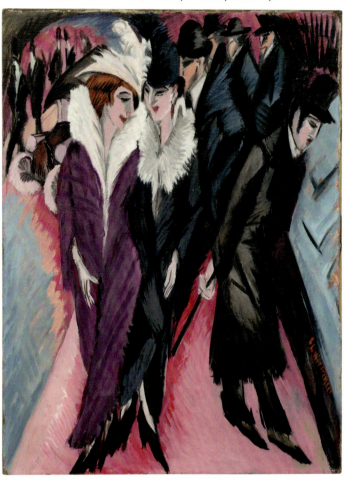

Ernst Kirchner was part of the German Expressionist group called Die Brücke, meaning "The Bridge." They felt their work bridged the German artists of the past with the bold styles of their time. You can spot the inspiration of modern movements, such as Fauvism (see room 98), in the painting's bright colors. Kirchner painted this work to show how big cities can feel glamorous, busy, and lonely all at once.

👁 How does this scene compare the scenes of city life on p.167?

MUSIC AND COLOR

WASSILY KANDINSKY, COMPOSITION VII, 1913

Wassily Kandinsky was part of the German Expressionist group Der Blaue Reiter, meaning "The Blue Rider." They believed colors had their own meanings. Kandinsky, for example, felt that yellow was energetic. He also thought paintings were similar to music, and used the musical term *composition* for some of his larger paintings. It may look like a wild mix of lines and colors, but Kandinsky made over thirty sketches before painting the final piece.

EXPRESSIVE WOODCUTS

KÄTHE KOLLWITZ, SELF-PORTRAIT, 1924

German Expressionist artists of the Die Brücke group were highly skilled in making woodcut prints. When Käthe Kollwitz discovered their work, she was inspired to create woodcut prints too. She had started her career making detailed works about war and the struggles of the poor, but in using woodcut printing, she had to simplify her complicated technique for the wooden blocks. After her son died in 1914, much of Kollwitz's artwork expressed her sadness.

Modern Art 173

ROOM 97

AMERICAN REGIONALISM
A Simple Life

During the 1930s, the United States went through a time called the Great Depression when many people had very little money. Around this period, a lot of galleries and artists were in big cities, like New York. Their work showed urban life. The American Regionalism movement wanted to change this by celebrating the lives of rural people. The style looked back to a simpler and happier time before the Great Depression.

MIDWESTERN MYSTERY

GRANT WOOD, AMERICAN GOTHIC, 1930

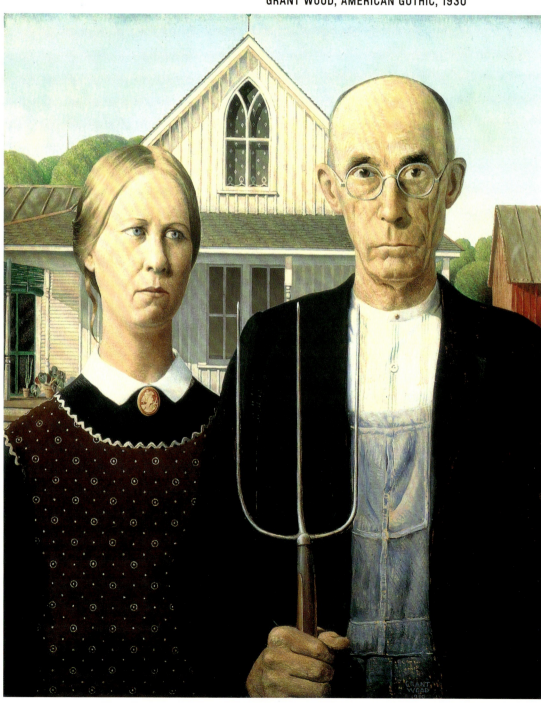

This painting shows an old-fashioned way of life that was disappearing as American cities became more modern. The name, *American Gothic*, refers to the window behind the two figures, which is pointed like old Gothic arches (see room 36). Grant Wood was inspired by a real house in his home state of Iowa, a house that still stands today. Wood was interested in the house because he thought the pointed Gothic window was an unusual architectural feature to find in the American Midwest. For the painting, he imagined a farmer and daughter who might live in that kind of house in the 1800s. When he needed models, he used his sister and their dentist!

👁 What similarities do you notice with this painting and the photograph by Gordon Parks in the next room?

174 The Ultimate Art Museum

AMERICAN PHOTOGRAPHY
Life on Film

ROOM 98

The first ever photograph taken was a blurry view out of a window, printed in 1827. Cameras were heavy, expensive, and not easy to carry around. The subject also had to be still for hours to get a clear picture!

Slowly, the technology got better and cameras became smaller. By the 1900s, artists could take photos more easily, and photography was used as a way to capture the world and all that was happening in it.

TRUE TO LIFE
GORDON PARKS, AMERICAN GOTHIC (ELLA WATSON), 1942

Gordon Parks was the first Black photographer at *LIFE*, a popular magazine known for its high-quality photography. When Parks moved to Washington, DC, in 1942, he was shocked by how unfairly Black people were treated there. Parks decided to photograph people's experiences. This picture of a cleaner called Ella Watson looks similar to Grant Wood's *American Gothic*. Just like the American Regionalism movement, Parks wanted to show another side of American life.

AN ICONIC MOTHER
DOROTHEA LANGE, MIGRANT MOTHER, 1936

This is the most famous photograph showing the Great Depression and the difficulties people faced. The photograph shows a Native American woman named Florence Owens Thompson. She and her family moved around to find work on farms, but there weren't many jobs during the Depression. Photographer Dorothea Lange captures the exhaustion of a mother as she sits with her children.

Modern Art 175

ROOM 99

BLACK-AMERICAN NARRATIVES
Representing Black Stories

There is not a single style of Black art. In fact, you'll find works by Black artists across this museum. The art in this room shows the blossoming creativity and changing lives of Black Americans after slavery was abolished in 1865. From 1916, many Black Americans left the South to escape racism and find jobs in the North and West. The Black arts that flourished in New York around this time are called the Harlem Renaissance.

A FIGHTER FOR FREEDOM
WILLIAM H. JOHNSON, HARRIET TUBMAN, c.1945

Harriet Tubman was one tough woman! She was born into slavery in the American South and ran away to the North for freedom. She then returned to the South 19 times to rescue 300 more people! William H. Johnson painted this portrait, as well as a series called Fighters for Freedom, to share the rich stories of Black Americans.

BOY IN BRONZE
AUGUSTA SAVAGE, GAMIN, c.1929

Augusta Savage started making small clay sculptures when she was a little girl. When she grew up, she decided she wanted to be an artist, and she moved from Florida to New York City. People loved this bronze bust of a gamin (a boy living on the streets) so much that Savage earned a scholarship to study in Europe. After this, she returned home to become a celebrated sculptor and important leader in the Harlem art community in New York.

GREAT LEADERS

JACOB LAWRENCE, SELF-PORTRAIT, 1977

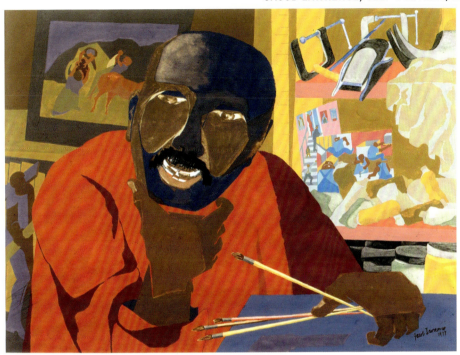

When Jacob Lawrence was 16 years old, he started taking free art lessons at the Harlem Art Workshop. There, he learned from Harlem Renaissance artists, such as Augusta Savage (see opposite page). From early on, Lawrence's art had bright colors and distinct shapes and patterns. He called his style Dynamic Cubism. He painted pictures that told the stories of great Black American leaders and reflected the everyday lives of Black people. This self-portrait shows Lawrence in his studio. You can spot some of his paintings in the background, including an image of Harriet Tubman (see opposite page) aiding enslaved people to freedom.

BEYOND THE BLANKET

HARRIET POWERS, BIBLE SCENES QUILT, 1886

A quilt can be more than a blanket to snuggle up to. It can tell a story and it can be art! Harriet Powers was born into slavery and learned how to sew during her life on a plantation. After the Civil War and the abolishment of slavery, she and her family had their own farm. She exhibited her first quilt at a fair in 1886 and later started to sell them to help support her family. This quilt shows scenes from the Bible, including Adam and Eve, Noah, the animals of the ark, and many more.

ART DETECTIVE

Only two of Harriet Powers's pieces of art have survived! The other is called *Pictorial Quilt* and shows fifteen events and stories.

Modern Art 177

SUPREMATISM
Pure and Simple

Up to the 1910s, most artists made art about people or things. Russian artist Kazimir Malevich wanted to get away from showing the real world, so he decided to paint shapes. The name of this movement comes from his belief in the supremacy, or greatness of simple **forms**. Other artists joined the movement and exhibited their work around Europe. This geometric style influenced later movements, such as De Stijl.

THE SHAPE OF A THOUGHT

KAZIMIR MALEVICH, SUPREMATIST COMPOSITION: WHITE ON WHITE, 1918

Have you ever thought about different shades of white? Kazimir Malevich did! He painted a white square on top of this creamy square canvas. He thought it looked like the square was floating in an empty space. Malevich believed artists could still show emotions in their work with squares, circles, and a small number of colors. Can you spot the rough texture? Even though he uses two similar colors, Malevich gives the picture some added detail through his brushstrokes.

DE STIJL
Building Blocks of Art

ROOM 101

De Stijl isn't just any style, it's "The Style." That's what the name means in Dutch. The movement was led by the Dutch artists Theo van Doesburg and Piet Mondrian. It is easy to recognize because pictures are made of straight lines, grids, and a few basic colors. De Stijl artists felt their style was a pure form of art that celebrated the elements (lines and color) that could create *any* image.

BOLD LINES, BRIGHT LIGHTS

PIET MONDRIAN, BROADWAY BOOGIE-WOOGIE 1942–43

Have you ever looked at a city map and noticed how the streets meet and cross? When the Dutch artist Piet Mondrian moved to New York to escape the Second World War, he was inspired by the bright lights, busy streets and the boogie-woogie music he discovered. The squares of this painting recreate a musical rhythm, or beats, while the lines are laid out like the streets of New York. The colors are simple, including white and the primary colors of red, yellow, and blue.

Modern Art 179

INDIAN MODERNISM
Free to Create

ROOM 102

Indian modernism celebrates an India free from British rule. For hundreds of years, the British had colonized parts of the country, then ruled over the whole as "the Raj." Indian independence encouraged people to think: what should a "modern" India look like? Artists also pondered this. They experimented with traditional Indian painting, European styles, and mixed the two for a uniquely Indian style of modern art.

THE BENGAL SCHOOL

ABANINDRANATH TAGORE, BHARAT MATA, 1905

Abanindranath Tagore was one of the early leaders of Indian modern art. He started out by training in European styles, but became fascinated with Mughal miniature paintings (see room 56). He created a modern version of this style, which became a movement called the Bengal School. Bharat Mata shows 'Mother India' holding symbols of the nation, including rice, cloth, prayer beads, and a book. This painting would later represent the strength of India during its fight for freedom.

DEEP IN THOUGHT

AMRITA SHER-GIL, THREE WOMEN, 1935

Amrita Sher-Gil had a Hungarian mother, an Indian Sikh father, and studied art in Paris. All of this was influential to her art, which combined European oil painting and traditional Indian miniature painting styles. She painted many images of villagers when she moved to India after her studies. Her paintings often show women with different shades of beautiful brown skin. They typically look thoughtful, as the three women appear in this oil painting.

MEXICAN MURALISM
Celebrating Mexican History

In the 1910s, Mexico went through big changes in government. When things settled down, many people were still divided by different beliefs, but artistic creativity began to explode. The government asked artists to create large murals to help unite the people. These artworks on walls celebrated the ancient peoples of Mexico, such as the Olmecs, Maya, and Aztecs (see gallery K), as well as the Spanish and modern cultures.

KNOWLEDGE IS POWER

JOSÉ CLEMENTE OROZCO, PROMETHEUS, 1930

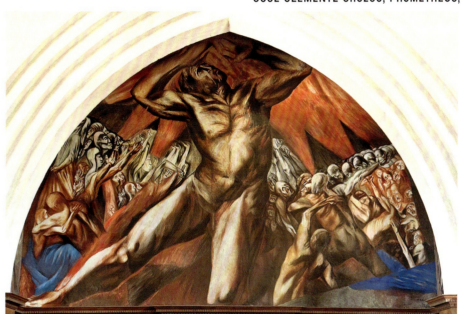

José Clemente Orozco was one of the key figures of Mexican muralism. He painted murals in the United States as well as Mexico. This mural is inspired by Greek mythology and the story of Prometheus, a Titan (one of the first gods) who stole fire from the heavens to give to humans. See how some figures in this painting are reaching for the fire while others appear afraid? The fire is thought to be a symbol for knowledge. What do you think Orozco could be telling us with this mural?

A MEXICAN FUTURE

DIEGO RIVERA, LIBERATED EARTH WITH NATURAL FORCES CONTROLLED BY MAN, 1926–27

This mural by Diego Rivera is painted in an assembly hall at the Universidad Autónoma Chapingo—a university in Mexico that specializes in the study of farming. The arched wall at the end shows a pregnant woman holding a small seedling. It is a symbol for earth. Around her are the natural elements of water, wind, and fire. To the front, Rivera shows figures using these natural elements alongside technology. It is a way of showing how Mexican people could use nature and science to create a bright future.

👁 Diego Rivera was the husband of the painter Frida Kahlo. Can you find her work in the Hall of Selfies?

Modern Art 181

ROOM 104

SURREALISM
Dream Worlds

Surrealist art shows real objects but in a completely fantastical way. It explores how dreams, imaginations and the inner workings of the mind can be shown in art. If you drew one of your dreams, it might look a little unusual too. French writer André Breton, who was once part of the Dada movement (see room 95), started Surrealism. It soon included artists all over the world!

CHUGGING DOWN THE CHIMNEY
RENÉ MAGRITTE, TIME TRANSFIXED, 1938

The Surrealists were excellent at mashing separate ideas together in a surprising way. René Magritte paints this train bursting through a fireplace as if it's moving through a tunnel. The smoke goes neatly up the inside of the fireplace as if it belongs there. Everything else in the room seems so normal, peaceful, and real. The artwork is nonsensical, and yet, it works.

HAIRY DRINKS!
MERET OPPENHEIM, OBJECT, 1936

Meret Oppenheim had the idea for this piece during a lunch with Pablo Picasso (see p.169) and the photographer Dora Maar. Picasso noticed Oppenheim's fur bracelets and said that almost anything could be covered in fur. She responded, "Even this cup and saucer?" Her response turned into a piece of art. Would you have a drink out of this furry cup? It might not be pleasant, but it could help keep a drink warm.

? ART DETECTIVE

Surrealists liked to play games to make art. This included a game in which they would draw part of a picture, fold it over, and pass it to another person to add to it. They couldn't look at what the last person drew, so these created very odd pictures! Why don't you try the game?

182 The Ultimate Art Museum

TIME MELTS

SALVADOR DALÍ, THE PERSISTENCE OF MEMORY, 1931

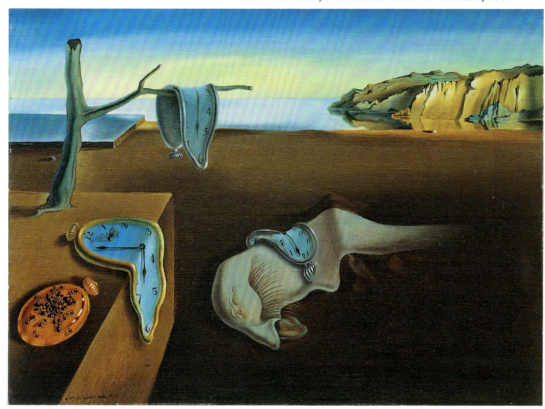

Clocks are full of solid, turning, and ticking bits that wouldn't usually fold and droop over things. But that's exactly what Spanish painter Salvador Dalí did here. He was inspired by the idea of cheese melting in the sun. The clock in the center is draped over part of a face. Can you see the long eyelashes on the closed eyelid? What bizarre dreams it must be having within this strange Surrealist dreamland!

👁 Dalí studied fantastical works by Hieronymus Bosch. See his work on p.124.

IMAGINED REALITIES

DOROTHEA TANNING, EINE KLEINE NACHTMUSIK, 1943

Dorothea Tanning was a writer and self-taught artist. This means she developed her art skills on her own rather than at school. Many of her fantastical paintings look like dreams that have come alive! Here, Tanning shows sunflowers as beastly creatures climbing up stairs into a hotel hallway. A young girl and a life-size doll (in the red jacket) seem to be battling an unseen force. This painting is named after a classical music piece called "A Little Night Serenade" by Mozart.

Modern Art 183

MODERN SCULPTURE
Unreal Shapes

ROOM 105

If our earlier galleries have taught us anything, it's that sculptures should be of recognizable subjects, like realistic statues of people, right? Not at all! Modern artists took those subjects and represented them in non-lifelike styles. This is called abstract art. The sculptures in this room show how sculptors used interesting lines and shapes to show familiar subjects, like a person, but in a totally new way.

PERFECTLY BALANCED
ISAMU NOGUCHI, KOUROS, 1944–45

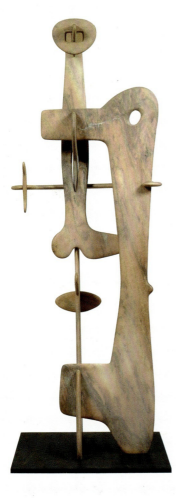

A *kouros* is an ancient sculpture of a male youth in ancient Greek art (see room 17). This large sculpture by the Japanese-American artist Isamu Noguchi is an abstract version of a *kouros*. Two large pieces of pink marble have been slotted together like puzzle pieces. It stays in place with the help of gravity and only two marble pins.

CARVING EMPTINESS
BARBARA HEPWORTH, TWO FIGURES (MENHIRS), 1954–55

The open spaces of this sculpture by Barbara Hepworth are just as interesting as the carved wood pieces. Empty areas of a sculpture or blank spaces on a picture are called **negative space**. Instead of adding to build the sculpture up, Hepworth removed material to reveal a shape. Suddenly what isn't there is as important as what is there! Hepworth was incredibly skilled at creating interesting sculptures with negative spaces. This one shows two abstract figures. The round shapes were inspired by ancient man-made stones called menhirs.

COLLAGE
Art from Scraps

ROOM 106

Have you ever cut up bits of paper and glued them to a sheet to make a design? If so, you've made a collage! The Cubists (see room 93) used this technique often. They glued scraps of newspaper, wallpaper, and other materials onto paintings. Artists from other movements carried on with this idea, making entire pictures from collages and eventually making collages using computers.

SUMMER IN HARLEM

ROMARE BEARDEN, SUMMERTIME, 1967

This collage shows a woman enjoying ice cream on a summer day in Harlem, New York. In 1965, Romare Bearden started experimenting with magazine and photo clippings to show scenes of Black-American life. Can you spot the three other figures in this work? There is a man sitting next to the woman and two people peeking through windows behind her. The central figure holds her cone like a microphone, which could be a link to a famous blues song titled "Summertime."

MESSAGE IN THE CUTTINGS

HANNAH HÖCH, CUT WITH THE DADA KITCHEN KNIFE THROUGH THE LAST WEIMAR BEER-BELLY CULTURAL EPOCH IN GERMANY, 1919

When a collage is made from photographs, it is called a **photomontage**. This was a popular technique with Dadaists (see room 95), and Hannah Höch was among the first artists to use it. Her work often had a message. Can you see the word *anti*, which means "against"? She places it next to political leaders that went against Dadaist art. In another section of this collage, she shows a map of where women could vote and puts her picture near it. This shows she supported the right for women to vote.

Modern Art 185

GALLERY R
Postmodern and Contemporary Art Since the Mid-20th Century

In this last gallery, anything goes! Art can be big enough to fill a room or be made from things lying around a room. It can be super lifelike or look like nothing you've ever seen in your life. The possibilities are as endless as your imagination!

Artists have a habit of constantly making new styles that are very different from what came before. Postmodernism is a time after modern art, when artists explored many styles that were different from the modernist styles in the last gallery. From the mid-1900s, artists challenged how art could look and worked with new materials and ways of making art. Although art historians give labels to these different styles and their unique qualities, it's good to remember that many of them were happening at the same time. This was an exciting time to be an artist!

Many of the artists you'll discover in this gallery are still working today. Art by living artists and art that was done in recent history is called contemporary art. As you go through this gallery, you will see how artists use art to express their feelings, test new ideas, and show the changing world around us.

ROOMS 107–28

Room	Title
107	EXPRESS YOURSELF
108	COLOR EVERYWHERE
109	LESS IS MORE
110	WHAT'S THE BIG IDEA?
111	NOT WHAT IT SEEMS
112	ART FOR EVERYONE
113	ANYTHING GOES
114	SURROUNDED BY ART
115	LIFE IN 3D
116	STITCH AND WEAVE
117	BRIGHT LIGHTS
118	THE GREAT OUTDOORS
119	ANCIENT STORIES, NEW ART
120	GIRL POWER
121	STANDING TOGETHER
122	MAKING A SCENE
123	ULTRA-REALISTIC PAINTINGS
124	CAUSE AND EFFECT
125	ACTING OUT
126	LIGHTS, CAMERA, ACTION!
127	PAINT WHAT'S INSIDE
128	HAPPENING NOW

186 The Ultimate Art Museum

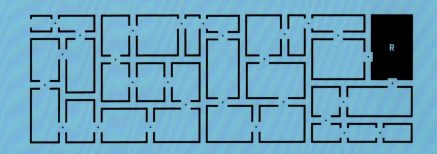

ART IS BORDERLESS

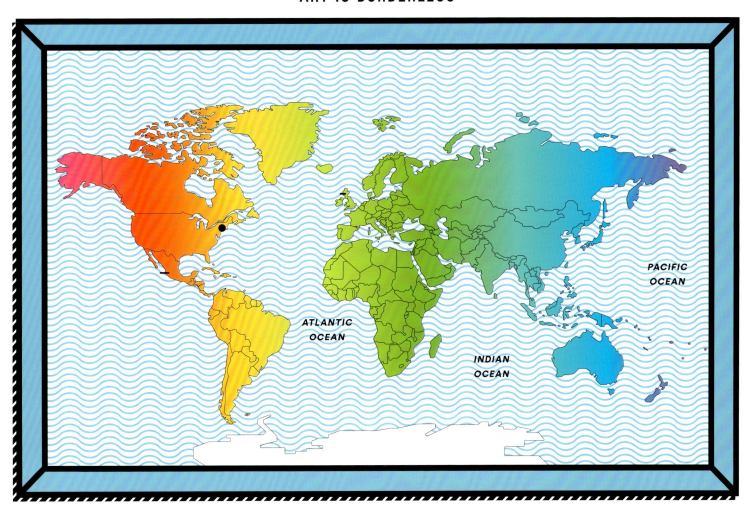

PEOPLE ARE MORE CONNECTED TO EACH OTHER THAN EVER BEFORE! SOME MOVEMENTS WERE INTERNATIONAL, AND ARTISTS ALL AROUND THE WORLD TRIED THEM. SOMETIMES ARTISTS WERE BORN IN ONE COUNTRY AND WORKED IN ANOTHER COUNTRY, GATHERING NEW IDEAS FROM DIFFERENT PLACES. ARTISTS NOW WORK ACROSS DIFFERENT COUNTRY BORDERS AND USE MANY DIFFERENT MEDIUMS AND STYLES.

ROOM 107

ABSTRACT EXPRESSIONISM
Express Yourself

Abstract Expressionism combines forms that are not realistic (abstract), and art that shows the artist's emotions (Expressionism). Some artists used splashes and dashes to paint a person or an object. Others created paintings that were **non-representational**, which means they don't show a person or object. Some made so-called action paintings—using actions, like throwing paint, to put color on the canvas.

ABSTRACT LANDSCAPES

JOAN MITCHELL, SALUT TOM, 1979

This painting is big enough to cover an entire wall! Joan Mitchell layered colors onto the canvas with fat brushstrokes and dripping paint. Can you see how the yellow areas sit at the top like the sky, and the black and green are low to be the ground? It is on four large panels and makes a landscape.

ADVENTUROUS ART

LEE KRASNER, ANOTHER STORM, 1963

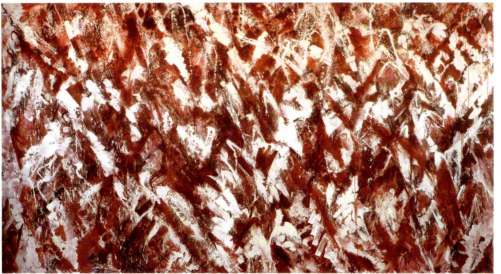

Lee Krasner was a key member of the Abstract Expressionists. She first trained in traditional and modern painting. She believed that artists should try new styles to make their work more exciting. Krasner was even known to rip up her own work when she didn't like it. The walls and floors of her studio were covered in splashes of color. This painting buzzes with energy because of her expressive brushes of paint.

188 The Ultimate Art Museum

SPLAT!

JACKSON POLLOCK, ONE: NUMBER 31, 1950

Jackson Pollock is famous for making a splash with his messy "action" paintings. He would lay massive canvases on the floor, then throw and drip the paint over the surface. Sometimes he left footprints on the canvas as he moved around! Pollock built up layers of color with different types of paints, including ordinary house paint.

HIDDEN LAYERS

WILLEM DE KOONING, WOMAN I, 1950–52

Do you notice what makes this painting different from Krasner and Pollock's paintings in this room? Willem de Kooning's painting shows a person, while the others are non-representational. De Kooning was inspired by Picasso's Cubist paintings of figures (see room 93), as well as the energetic brushstrokes in Pollock's action paintings. This piece is from his most famous series of paintings of women. It took two years to finish because De Kooning scraped and repainted areas many times. The canvas is covered in thick layers of paint. Some of the areas drip into each other or are applied so thinly they reveal layers underneath.

? ART DETECTIVE

Abstract Expressionism was the first big international art movement to begin in the United States. It began in the 1940s in New York City after the Second World War. It inspired so many artists that New York soon became one of the most important cities in which to make and discover art in the world.

COLOR FIELD
Color Everywhere

The fields in color field paintings aren't the kind you plant things in! They're "fields," or areas, of color painted onto canvases. Color field paintings used an abstract style that didn't show people, animals, or objects. Color itself was the star of the show! The paintings were often

made in huge sizes so that when a viewer stood in front of them, they felt like they were completely surrounded by the lively, bold colors.

GETTING SOAKED!

HELEN FRANKENTHALER, BLACK-EYED SUSAN, 1988

Helen Frankenthaler created her bold work by rolling out a massive canvas and splashing buckets of paint across the surface! The paints she used were thinned down, watery oil paints. She let them soak into the canvas like a colorful stain. Do you see how the stain technique leaves thinner layers of paint? It makes a very different effect to brushing thick oils onto a canvas. Take a look at Van Gogh's *Starry Night* (see p.164) to compare and contrast. This painting was inspired by the bold yellow, pink, and black colors found on the black-eyed Susan flower.

👁 Which other artists created work by using big actions such as throwing paint on a canvas? Hint: check out room 107.

Postmodern and Contemporary Art Since the Mid-20th Century

AN EMOTIONAL EXPERIENCE

MARK ROTHKO, HOMAGE TO MATISSE, 1954

Mark Rothko's colorful paintings were created to inspire emotional reactions from the viewer. Rothko painted huge pieces and encouraged people to stand very close so that they felt like they were inside the painting. On seeing his work, some people have burst into tears! Do you see how the edges of the colors are rough and blend into the yellow background? He worked by placing thin layers of paint on top of each other so that the colors beneath gently peek through.

PATTERNS OF COLOR

ALMA THOMAS, SPRINGTIME IN WASHINGTON, 1971

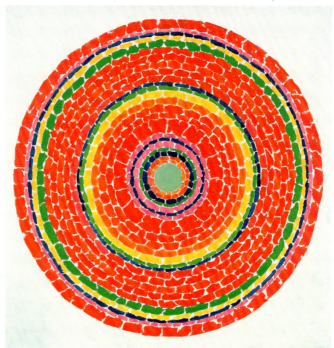

Alma Thomas studied art at Howard University, a historically Black school in the US, where her professors encouraged her to try painting in abstract styles. After graduating, she became a schoolteacher, and it was only when she retired that she began to experiment with her own style. Thomas grew interested in the color field movement and became famous when she first showed her work at the age of 75! *Springtime in Washington* shows Thomas's style of using short brushstrokes in bold colors that look like mosaics.

MINIMALISM
Less is More

ROOM 109

A 'minimum' is the least amount of something needed. Minimalist art is a style that uses very simple shapes and only a small number of colors. When describing the Minimalist movement, artist Frank Stella said, "What you see is what you see." This group of artists didn't try to paint things from the real world or show emotions with their art. They wanted people to simply think about the shapes and colors in front of them.

FLAT SHAPES

ELLSWORTH KELLY, RED BLUE GREEN, 1963

Ellsworth Kelly is most famous for his Minimalist paintings of bright and simple shapes. Do you notice in this painting how the edges are very crisp and there are no shadows? This makes them appear flat, rather than popping out in a three-dimensional way. Kelly's shapes are also not outlined. They stand out from each other because the colors are so different. Kelly was inspired by Cubist paintings (see room 93), which also had flat colors and shapes. He looked at things he saw in the real world, and used the fewest elements possible to create an interesting image of them.

? ART DETECTIVE

During the Second World War, Ellsworth Kelly belonged to the USA's Ghost Army, a unit of around 1,100 men who built and painted fake planes, tanks, and buildings. The aim was to trick the Nazi airplanes flying overhead into targeting the fake troops rather than the real ones that were elsewhere.

ROOM 110

CONCEPTUAL ART
What's the Big Idea?

A concept is an idea, so Conceptual art is all about big ideas in art! There are two main kinds to discover. In one, the artist creates art to explore an idea. The other is when an artist creates art to make *you* think. In these pieces, the viewer is an important part—what you think about the artwork helps decide what it means. Conceptual art can be any medium, including sculpture, painting, performance, and more.

SHARK!

DAMIEN HIRST, THE PHYSICAL IMPOSSIBILITY OF DEATH IN THE MIND OF SOMEONE LIVING, 1991

Yes, that is a real shark. No, it isn't alive. This is one of Damien Hirst's most famous artworks, showing a tiger shark. It is floating in a tank of formaldehyde, which is a preserving liquid. The shark is frozen in a fearsome position with its mouth open and ready to chomp! Hirst planned his artworks with the help of scientists so that the preserving liquid was just right. He is curious about life and death, so many of his works try to make people think about these ideas.

MAKE A PLAN

SOL LEWITT, OPEN MODULAR CUBE, 1966

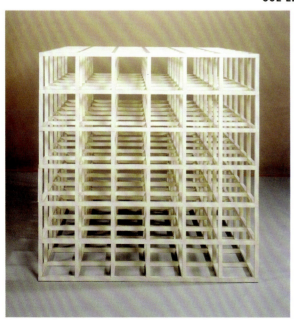

In the 1960s, Sol LeWitt had the idea to create sculptures made of cubes. *Open Modular Cube* is one big cube made from many smaller cubes. As viewers move around it, the lines of the open cubes cross each other and create interesting shapes and effects. LeWitt made many different sculptures he called "structures," using these cubes like building blocks. He said that Conceptual artists should plan out their ideas before starting to make them into art.

? ART DETECTIVE

Sol LeWitt sold wall drawings that he never made himself! Instead, he gave detailed instructions on how to make the drawings, with a signed sheet of paper to prove it was really his idea.

194 The Ultimate Art Museum

OP ART
Not What it Seems

ROOM 111

Don't be fooled by what you see! Op Art uses optical illusions to trick the eye. Artists use lines, colors, and shapes in clever ways, including making patterns to create images that look like they are moving or blurring.

This technique can also be used to make a three-dimensional shape appear on a flat **two-dimensional** surface. The longer you look, the more interesting they become!

DIFFERENT ANGLES

JESÚS RAFAEL SOTO, SPHERE LUTECIA, 1995

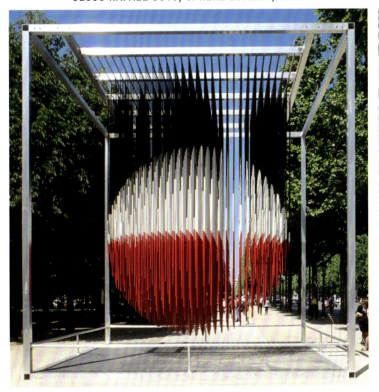

This sculpture by Jesús Rafael Soto changes as you walk around it. If you stand at one end, it simply looks like neat hanging rows with a circular design. When you walk around, the spaces between the bars appear to change positions and move. Soto often uses lines or bars that are hanging or sticking up from the floor in his art. By doing this, a sculpture can change with the movement of wind, while floor sculptures change as people move around and see the artwork from different angles.

👁 Soto's sculpture looks like a sphere hanging in the sky. Where else can you spot geometric shapes in art in this wing?

ENERGETIC LINES

BRIDGET RILEY, FALL, 1963

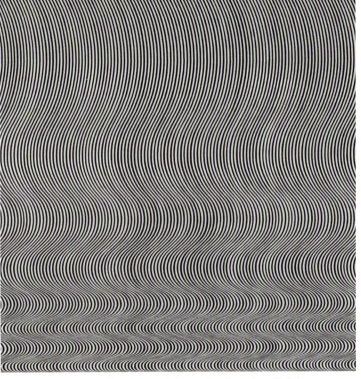

The longer you look at this painting by Bridget Riley, the more it appears to vibrate and slide across the surface. The effect is even stronger if you don't focus your eyes on it. Do you notice how the lines become slightly thinner at the curved parts? This gives the pattern a three-dimensional effect, like rippling fabric. Riley was one of the lead artists of the Op Art movement. She was extremely skilled at putting shapes and lines together in energetic designs that really fool the eye.

👁 Can you create your own Op Art? Try drawing lines far apart and close together to see what effects you can create.

Postmodern and Contemporary Art Since the Mid-20th Century

ROOM 112

POP ART
Art for Everyone

Have you ever picked up a tin of soup and thought, "This looks like a great piece of art?" In the 1950s, artists did just that. Pop is short for *popular* because this movement is inspired by popular things, such as comics, movies, and shop items. Some artists used styles that were typically used for newspapers and product packaging. The Pop artists thought everyday items were just as artistic as any object in a gallery!

POW!

ROY LICHTENSTEIN, WHAAM!, 1963

Does this painting look like a scene from a comic? That's because it is one! Roy Lichtenstein based his artwork on panels from *All-American Men of War* by DC Comics. Even though he hand-painted the image, Lichtenstein recreated the dots (called Ben-Day dots), which used to appear on machine-printed materials, such as newspapers and comics. Advertisements and comics were not seen as pieces of artwork that belonged in a gallery until Lichtenstein challenged that idea.

ICONIC CANS

ANDY WARHOL, CAMPBELL'S SOUP CANS, 1962

Andy Warhol was very curious about the idea of fame and loved to feature celebrities and popular brands in his artwork. One of his best-known artwork series is of Campbell soup cans. Do you notice how each of these 32 paintings seem identical? Warhol did this intentionally because he was interested in the printing techniques that were used to make shop products look exactly the same. He used stamps to make the gold pattern at the bottom and painted the rest by hand.

CANNONBALL!

**DAVID HOCKNEY,
A BIGGER SPLASH, 1967**

From a very young age, David Hockney loved to doodle and make art. When he moved to Los Angeles, he became interested in painting the city landscapes that were so different from his home in Britain. He created a series of swimming pool paintings in which he explored different effects in the blue water. *A Bigger Splash* is a moment frozen in time, just after someone has jumped in the pool.

BEGINNING IN BRITAIN

RICHARD HAMILTON, JUST WHAT IS IT THAT MAKES TODAY'S HOMES SO DIFFERENT, SO APPEALING?, 1956

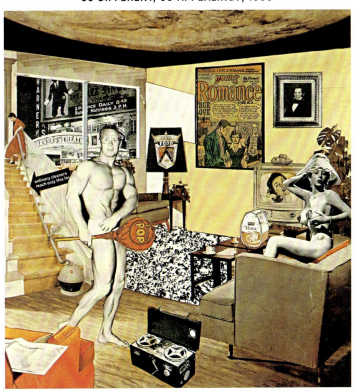

This collage by British artist Richard Hamilton was one of the first major Pop artworks. In the image, Hamilton creates a 1950s dream home using pictures cut out of American magazines. It is filled with popular items, such as comics, and products like the giant Tootsie Pop the bodybuilder is holding. Many of the items might look old to us now, but they were ultra-modern at the time!

EYE-POPPING WORDS

ROBERT INDIANA, LOVE, 1966

Robert Indiana was fascinated by signs, advertisements, and images about life in the US. Many of Indiana's paintings and sculptures show short words or numbers. This image of the word *Love* is his most famous. Does this remind you of a sign you might see outside a shop? The first version of this piece was designed as a Christmas card for the Museum of Modern Art in New York in 1965. Since then, it has been recreated on prints, stamps, the sculpture you see here, and more.

? ART DETECTIVE

Robert Indiana was in a film by Andy Warhol called *Eat*. It's a black-and-white movie with no sound, showing him eating a mushroom for 40 minutes! He only takes a break to cuddle a cat.

ROOM 113
UNUSUAL MATERIALS
Anything Goes

For thousands of years, sculptures were made from a common set of materials, like wood, clay, or stone. When the Dada artists (see room 95) came along in the 1910s, they showed the world that sculptures could be made from anything—even a toilet! Since then, artists have used more and more unusual materials to create sculptures. When artists put together existing objects to create new artworks, these are called assemblages.

A WINDOW TO THE SOUL
BETYE SAAR, BLACK GIRL'S WINDOW, 1969

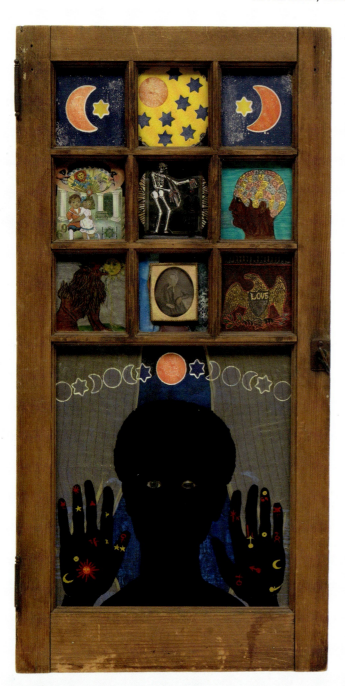

Betye Saar is known for assemblages that play with themes of magic and subjects that relate to Black-American life. This one is made from an old window frame. Here, the figure looks like she is pressing her hands against imaginary glass. This gives the feeling that she is trapped and looking out at the viewer. The eyes are the only visible facial feature on the shadowy person, as eyes are often referred to as the window to the soul.

COOL COMBINATIONS
ROBERT RAUSCHENBERG, MONOGRAM, 1955–59

Robert Rauschenburg used a mixture of techniques and everyday materials to create assemblages and artworks. Rauschenberg called this type of artwork a "Combine" because it combines paintings and objects together. *Monogram* is one of his most famous Combines. The bottom is made of newspapers and old signs. Rauschenburg paid $15 to buy the stuffed goat from a second-hand shop, so he could put the tyre around its waist.

INSTALLATION ART
Surrounded by Art

ROOM 114

Installations are impressive artworks that can be as big as a building! They are designed to transform a space, such as a room in an art gallery, into a work of art. Some installations are large enough for people to walk inside, while others can be a single sculpture or even an image projected onto a wall. The most important thing is that the artwork transforms an area into an interesting place with a new experience.

INSIDE-OUT

RACHEL WHITEREAD, HOUSE, 1993

Have you ever thought about what the empty space in a room might look like if it were solid? For this huge installation, Rachel Whiteread filled a three-story house in London with concrete! It created an inside-out shape of the empty building and brought the negative space to life. Transforming the house like this meant that even after its walls were torn down, it still existed through the solid empty space.

👁 For another artistic interpretation of a house visit p.208.

UNREADABLE TEXT

XU BING, BOOK FROM THE SKY, c.1987–1991

Book from the Sky by Xu Bing is an installation covering a room in 4,000 Chinese characters (symbols used for writing). The characters are neatly printed on long sheets that droop from the ceiling, ripple across the floor, and hang from the walls. But there's just one catch. All of the words are made up! Bing took different parts of real Chinese characters and mixed them up to create nonsense words that look believable. The installation displays the pages like they are a precious, sacred text, but really they're full of words that no one can read! Like much of Bing's work, this installation asks viewers to think about the importance of written language.

ZOOM IN

Postmodern and Contemporary Art Since the Mid-20th Century

CONTEMPORARY SCULPTURE
Life in 3D

A contemporary sculpture can be almost any 3D artwork. Sculptors in the first half of the 1900s (see room 105) used traditional materials, like wood and marble, to make abstract work. The sculptors that came later built on these ideas by trying out completely different materials. Today, sculptures can be made from many things and can even have moving parts. Contemporary sculptures can hang on a wall or be as big as a house.

A MONUMENTAL MIRROR
ANISH KAPOOR, CLOUD GATE, 2004–06

This gigantic sculpture by Anish Kapoor weighs about as much as a blue whale! It was made as shiny as a mirror, so that it can reflect the viewer. Simply by looking at the surface, the viewer becomes part of the art. It is made from 168 steel plates that were joined together and polished until the sculpture became mirrored and the seams disappeared. It was created to go in Millennium Park in Chicago, USA.

> **ART DETECTIVE**
>
> Anish Kapoor is known for creating works that feature the colors red and black. He likes black so much that he went in search of the blackest black in the world!

FINDING GOLD
LOUISE NEVELSON, ROYAL TIDE–DAWN, 1960

Louise Nevelson created massive, abstract sculptures made from "found objects." Using existing objects to make sculptures was a huge change from carving artworks from raw materials. Nevelson's sculptures sometimes included pieces of furniture, wood, and metal that were fitted together like a puzzle and painted the same color. This sculpture is from a series called Royal Tide, with all of the pieces painted to look golden. She was inspired to use gold as it can be found throughout nature, such as the bright golden light of the sun.

NATURE'S WEAVERS

LOUISE BOURGEOIS, SPIDER, 1997

Louise Bourgeois is known for spider sculptures that are not so itsy-bits—in fact, they're massive! Bourgeois's spider sculptures were inspired by her mother, who was a weaver. Spiders are the weavers of the animal world. The spider in this sculpture could be a mother protecting her young or a hunter eating its prey. Inside the weblike cage, the items, such as tapestries and a favorite perfume, have a special meaning for Bourgeois.

👁 Where there's a spider, there's a web! Go to p.211 to see a web so realistic it looks like it could catch flies.

FIELDS OF STEEL

DAVID SMITH, FIELD INSTALLATION, c.1960

David Smith's studio was on a farm, where he would sometimes set sculptures out in rows like they were crops growing from the earth. Smith is known for creating huge, abstract sculptures of steel. He first learned how to join heavy metals together by working in a car factory, and used these techniques to make his towering sculptures. This group of tall, twisting shapes was placed in a field in New York state.

ART ON THE MOVE

ALEXANDER CALDER, OTTO'S MOBILE, 1952

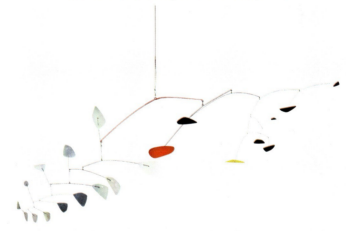

Did you know that the mobile was first invented by the artist Alexander Calder in the early 1930s? A mobile is a type of abstract sculpture. Colorful shapes balance delicately on thin wires that allow parts of the sculpture to spin and twist. Marcel Duchamp (see p.171) gave these great works of art the name "mobiles," which means "motive" and "motion" in French. A sculpture that has moving parts is called a kinetic sculpture.

Postmodern and Contemporary Art Since the Mid-20th Century 201

TEXTILE ART
Stitch and Weave

ROOM 116

Textiles are all around us! They're the rugs we walk on, the clothes we wear, and any other type of cloth or woven material. For a long time, textiles were seen as "crafts," and people didn't think they belonged in galleries. In the modern era, that changed. Artists brought back ancient techniques and used traditional materials with modern styles and ideas to show how special textiles were in art.

ADVENTURES AT THE MUSEUM
FAITH RINGGOLD, DANCING AT THE LOUVRE, 1991

This artwork tells the story of a character named Willia Marie Simone, a young Black American woman who moves to Paris and has many adventures. The quilt shows Willia and her friends dancing in front of Leonardo da Vinci's *Mona Lisa* at the Louvre Museum. It's the first of twelve quilts in a series called the French Collection. In other quilts, Willia continues her adventures to meet famous people such as Pablo Picasso (see p.169) and Rosa Parks. Faith Ringgold, is loved for using traditional Black quilting techniques to "paint" with fabrics. Her artworks show creative stories of groups, like women and Black people, who have often been left out of historical writings.

👁 This quilt shows Leonardo da Vinci's *Mona Lisa*. Can you find another painting by him in wing two?

SHOWING OFF
ANNI ALBERS, BLACK WHITE YELLOW, 1926/1964

When Anni Albers studied at the famous Bauhaus art school in Germany, women artists were only allowed to learn certain techniques, so Albers chose weaving. But that didn't stop her from trying new designs. Albers made wall hangings like *Black White Yellow* and called them "pictorial weavings." They were woven artworks meant to be shown and not used. Her way of weaving was so new and exciting that Albers became the first textile artist to have a solo exhibition at the Museum of Modern Art in New York.

202 The Ultimate Art Museum

WORKING WITH LIGHT
Bright Lights

ROOM 117

Light was important for Impressionist artists (see room 87) who looked at how different lighting from the sun could change how they painted something. In the 1900s, artists began to take control of light and use it as art. Bulbs of different colors and sizes could be shone onto a space in an interesting way. Lights were also used to write messages with neon signs. Both the light source and the glow bouncing off a surface could become art!

USE YOUR WORDS

JENNY HOLZER, FOR CHICAGO, 2007

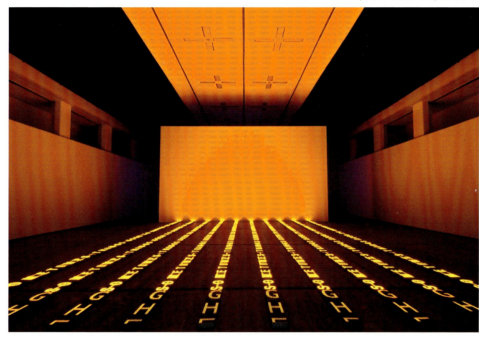

This photograph shows a row of LED strips with scrolling messages. Holzer often uses LED light strips, which produce light from electricity. She uses these strips to share her thoughts about people and politics. Similar kinds of strips are used to tell everyone the news in public spaces. This makes the messages in Holzer's work seem like they could be coming from an official source, like a newspaper.

👁 Text can be very powerful in art. Go to pp.61, 107, 185, 196, 197, 199, 209 to see how other artists have used writing in their work.

LIGHT SCULPTURES

DAN FLAVIN, THE NOMINAL THREE (TO WILLIAM OF OCKHAM), 1963

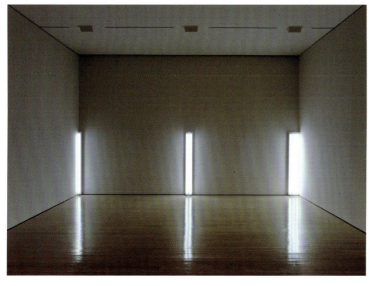

Dan Flavin uses everyday fluorescent tube lights to create spaces that glow. These types of lights are usually used in public buildings like shops or schools, but Flavin turns them into artworks. His light artworks are minimalist (see room 109) sculptures. The title of the artwork celebrates William of Ockham, who was a philosopher in the 1300s. The philosopher said that when someone has lots of different ideas to choose from, the simplest option is the best one to take. This artwork shows the simple idea of counting to three. To the left is one bulb, then two and then three—how simple!

👁 What other artwork includes everyday materials?

Postmodern and Contemporary Art Since the Mid-20th Century

ROOM 117

FLOATING AMONG LIGHTS

YAYOI KUSAMA, FIREFLIES ON THE WATER, 2002

When Japanese artist Yayoi Kusama was little, she imagined that she saw a field of flowers speak to her. She felt that she was disappearing into an endless field of dots. This memory has inspired her to use lights, dots, and mirrors to create spaces that feel endless. In this room-sized installation, 150 small LED lights hang from the ceiling. Walking into this room is like floating among the stars in space. Have you been in a room surrounded by mirrors? Remember how your reflection multiplies and looks like it goes on forever? This room has mirrored walls and a pool of water in the center so that the glimmering lights in the room are multiplied. Viewers walk onto a platform in the room to be surrounded by the installation. People have been known to get so caught up in the beauty of the artwork that they have walked off the platform and into the pool!

Postmodern and Contemporary Art Since the Mid-20th Century

LAND ART
The Great Outdoors

Imagine huge outdoor sculptures made from piles of rocks, or complex pictures dug into the earth! Land artists created works to encourage people to think about the environment and how people interact with nature. Some used natural materials, such as rocks and wood. Other artists, such as Christo and Jeanne-Claude, used artificial materials in a natural landscape to emphasize the environment.

COVERING A COAST
CHRISTO AND JEANNE-CLAUDE, WRAPPED COAST, ONE MILLION SQUARE FEET, 1968–69

Christo and Jeanne-Claude were artists, and husband and wife, who created massive outdoor installations. They began in 1958 by wrapping objects, such as oil barrels, in canvas cloth. The size of the objects grew until they were wrapping buildings and then an entire coastline! This photograph shows a stretch of the Australian coast that they briefly covered in fabric. They had to get the help of architects and mountain climbers to tie the material down to the rocky cliffs. The project took four weeks to complete. It was up for ten weeks before the coast was restored to its original state. Christo and Jeanne-Claude liked to create artworks that were only displayed for a short time. This was a way they could use art to show that things don't last forever.

ABORIGINAL AUSTRALIAN ART
Ancient Stories, New Art

ROOM 119

Aboriginal Australians are the native peoples of Australia and include more than 400 cultural groups. There are many artists today who use traditional Aboriginal styles to make paintings and sculptures. This room displays sacred animals called *mimi*, which are mythical figures that teach important lessons or can even trick people. Using art to celebrate ancient stories means that they continue to be passed on through the generations.

THE KANGAROO CREATOR

JOHNNY LIWANGU, GARRTJAMBAL KANGAROO AND THE STORY OF THE NORTH-EAST WIND, 1989

This painting by Johnny Liwangu shows a sacred kangaroo called Garrtjambal. Next to him is the Rainbow Serpent. Myths of these two creatures come from Dreamtime, which describes Aboriginal spiritual beliefs and the beginning of life. Liwangu works in styles similar to ancient Australian rock paintings and uses natural pigments, too.

STANDING STRONG

PADDY DHATANGU, GEORGE MILPURRURRU, DAVID MALANGI, JIMMY WULULU AND OTHER RAMINGINING ARTISTS, ABORIGINAL MEMORIAL, 1987–88

This memorial was created by 43 men living in an Aboriginal Australian community called Ramingining. It includes 200 logs, called *dupun*, which represent sacred coffins for bones. Here, the *dupun* are a symbol for each year that the Aboriginal people have lost their lives because of the arrival of European colonizers. Each log has designs and sacred animals that relate to different Aboriginal clans. Although the memorial was made to remember a period of sadness and loss, it also shows how the Aboriginal groups still stand strong and continue to pass on their rich heritage to new generations.

FEMINIST ART
Girl Power

ROOM 120

Feminism is the belief that everyone should be treated equally, whether they are a man, woman, or non-binary. For thousands of years, women weren't treated the same as men; they could not vote in elections or do certain jobs. Lots of women across the world came together to protest against unfair treatment. Beginning in the 1960s, women artists created art that celebrated women and promoted equality for all.

AN EPIC PARTY
JUDY CHICAGO, THE DINNER PARTY, 1974–79

In this installation, Judy Chicago created a fantasy dinner party that imagines 39 incredible women from history sitting around a table. The guests include artists like Georgia O'Keeffe and Artemisia Gentileschi (see p.131, 154), as well as historical figures, such as Sojourner Truth, who fought for equal rights for women and African-Americans. Each woman has her own special place setting that represents who she is.

> **ART DETECTIVE**
>
> Judy Chicago got the inspiration for this installation after she went to a real dinner party at which only the men spoke.

AN UNUSUAL HOUSE
MIRIAM SCHAPIRO, DOLLHOUSE, 1972

At first, *Dollhouse* looks like an ordinary toy, but Miriam Schapiro has made unexpected changes. A monster waits in the baby's room and a bear looks through the top floor window! In the artist's studio, Schapiro puts in one of her own paintings. The areas that people thought were for women, like the baby's room and kitchen, are scary. But the art studio, which was once thought to be for men, belongs to a woman artist. Schapiro did this to shake up old ideas about what women and girls can do.

208 The Ultimate Art Museum

CHICANX ART
Standing Together

ROOM 121

Chicanx refers to both "Chicano" men and "Chicana" women. It is how some Mexican-Americans refer to themselves. This art movement began in the 1960s, when Chicanx people protested against racism and unfair working conditions. Chicanx artists encouraged people to be proud of their brown skin and rich Mexican-American heritage. Their work includes artistic influences from popular Mexican and American culture.

BIG DREAMS
CARMEN LOMAS GARZA, CAMAS PARA SUEÑOS, 1985

When Carmen Lomas Garza was a little girl, she was inspired by the Chicanx movement and became an artist who showed everyday Mexican-American life. This painting shows Garza and her sister sitting on their roof and fantasizing about becoming artists. Through the window, you can see their mother making their beds inside. Many of her paintings are based on her experiences of growing up in Texas.

SNACK ATTACK
ESTER HERNANDEZ, SUN MAD, 1982

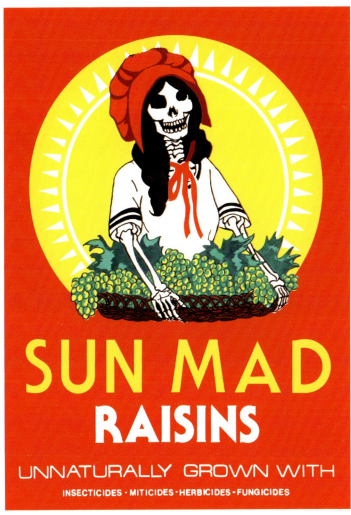

Ester Hernandez grew up in a small farming town in a grape-growing area of California. She saw how many Chicanx farmers protested for better treatment, and this inspired her later art. When her mother told her about how the drinking water in her hometown was being made unsafe by pesticides, she created this artwork. She replaces the happy grape picker on the Sun Maid logo with a skeleton and changes the words to show that the farms used unsafe chemicals.

Postmodern and Contemporary Art Since the Mid-20th Century

PHOTOGRAPHY TODAY
Making a Scene

ROOM 122

Photography doesn't have to show real life. Artists sometimes create dazzling scenes with invented characters to tell a story. As technology has improved over time, some photographers choose to edit photos in a **darkroom** or on a computer. They can add things in that were never there, change the colors, or stitch together different photographs. It's like collage, except it looks as if what you see really happened.

OPPOSING IDEAS

SHIRIN NESHAT, UNTITLED (RAPTURE) FROM THE SERIES RAPTURE, 1999

Shirin Neshat is an Iranian photo and video artist. She likes to create scenes that encourage people to think about two opposite ideas, such as how men and women are thought of differently. For her Rapture series, Neshat photographed Muslim women and men in two separate groups. The men are shown in buildings and the women (as seen here) are shown in nature. By showing two different ideas in the series, she encourages you to think about the similarities and differences between people, and why those differences might exist.

BLOWN AWAY

JEFF WALL, A SUDDEN GUST OF WIND (AFTER HOKUSAI), 1993

This photograph by Jeff Wall captures the moment when a gust of wind sweeps a businessman's papers from his hands. Although it looks like it was taken quickly in the moment, it's actually several different photographs that were combined together. This photo is inspired by a print by the Japanese artist Katsushika Hokusai (see room 85) titled *Ejiri in Suruga Province*. Wall creates photographs inspired by art history to help us think about images from the past in a new way.

👁 What other artists were inspired by Japanese prints? Go to room 86.

PAINTING IN THE AGE OF PHOTOGRAPHY
Ultra-Realistic Paintings

ROOM 123

For thousands of years, paintings and sculptures were the only ways to record how a person looked. When photography was invented in the 1800s, it was less important for paintings to do this job. But that doesn't mean that artists stopped making lifelike paintings! In fact, some became even more realistic. The paintings in this room look so real that you'll have to look twice to believe they aren't photographs.

FATHER AND DAUGHTER
GERHARD RICHTER, BETTY, 1988

PICTURING NATURE
VIJA CELMINS, WEB #3, 2000–2002

Gerhard Richter is fascinated by the way photographs can capture memories and history. Cameras take pictures just as they happen. Richter likes to think like a camera by showing scenes just as they are. This painting is based on a photograph of his 11-year-old daughter, Betty, and doesn't include any personal touches that might show that it was painted by her father. The texture of her clothing and the details of her thin strands of hair are extremely realistic.

Vija Celmins creates extremely lifelike paintings of nature, based on photographs. Her work is often black-and-white and shows interesting textures, such as waves and rocks. This painting shows the thin, delicate lines of a spider web. Celmins says the process of drawing and painting is very important to her, so we can imagine that she put just as much care into painting this web as the spider that built it!

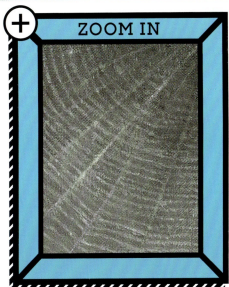

ZOOM IN

DECOLONIZING ART
Cause and Effect

ROOM 124

Many cultures have been affected by colonization, which is when a group of people—or a country—invades and rules over another group of people who are already there. This has caused negative effects, as many people have been forced to change or leave their native lands. To "decolonize" something is to undo these destructive changes. The works in this room inspire viewers to think about colonization and its effect on people.

OUR SHARED PAST
YINKA SHONIBARE CBE, LEISURE LADY (WITH OCELOTS), 2001

Where do our traditions come from? The British-Nigerian artist Yinka Shonibare makes sculptures that challenge people to think about where different parts of our cultures began. He uses **wax print** fabrics worn in many West African cultures. These fabrics were influenced by Indonesian designs and brought to Africa by British and Dutch colonialists. In this sculpture, Shonibare plays with the idea of multiculturalism (belonging to different cultures) by showing a woman wearing British Victorian-style dress made with African wax prints. She is walking three ocelots.

CHALLENGING IDEAS
KARA WALKER, DANSE DE LA NUBIENNE NOUVEAUX (DETAIL), 1998

Kara Walker isn't afraid to create art that makes people uncomfortable. Many of her works show the horrible story of slavery and racism in America. This installation uses black paper cutouts of women leaping and dancing through the air as though they are witches, highlighting one of the many negative and untrue ideas people once had about Black women. Walker asks us to think about how Black women have been treated from the time of colonialism up to the present day.

👁 Art can be a powerful way to tackle negative ideas. Visit p.167 to see how another artist challenged unfair stereotypes.

PERFORMANCE ART
Acting Out

ROOM 125

Performance art is when a person or group uses actions to create an artwork. This can be a simple action, like one artist pushing a block of ice down the street, or can involve lots of people, like a play with many actors.

These artworks are often a type of Conceptual art (see room 110). They can ask the viewer to think deeply about an idea by experiencing something new and interesting.

SOMETHING FOR NOTHING
FRANCIS ALŸS, PARADOX OF PRAXIS I, 1997

When artists spend time on a project, you might expect to see an exciting object at the end. Well, not after Francis Alÿs made this piece of art. The artist started the performance with a big block of ice, but it disappeared as he pushed it around Mexico City for nine hours. This is why the longer title for this work includes the phrase, "Sometimes Doing Something Leads to Nothing." That's the opposite of what you might expect from the process of creating art! The performance took place in Mexico because Alÿs wanted viewers to think about the hard and frustrating work many Latin Americans have to do in order to earn enough money to live. The idea shows that even after all of their work, sometimes the money they earn isn't enough.

👁 What other works in this gallery were made to highlight bad conditions for workers?

Postmodern and Contemporary Art Since the Mid-20th Century

ROOM 126

VIDEO ART
Lights, Camera, Action!

Artists first began making video art in the 1960s, when home recording equipment became cheaper and easier to buy. Unlike a film you might watch in a theater, video art doesn't always need to tell a story or have actors. These artworks can record performance art (see room 125) or can be another way to display an image, like a digital canvas for art. Video art is often shown on TV screens or projected onto an art gallery's walls.

FLOWER POWER

PIPILOTTI RIST, EVER IS OVER ALL, 1997

The film *Ever is Over All* begins with a woman walking down a street in slow motion with a big smile on her face. She carries a flower with a long stem as she walks and holds it high like an Olympian carrying a torch. Suddenly, she takes the flower and begins smashing car windows! It's all destructive and happy at the same time. Rist is known for creating playful videos in which women take center stage.

? ART DETECTIVE

In 2016, the singer Beyoncé was inspired by Pipilotti Rist's video artwork *Ever is Over All* for her music video for "Hold Up."

THE FIRST VIDEO ARTIST

NAM JUNE PAIK, VIDEO FLAG, 1985–96

Nam June Paik is the founder of video art. He started by using old recordings and as he created more video art, he filmed some of his own recordings too. *Video Flag* shows many television sets with colorful screens arranged in the pattern of the American flag. The blue screens change between images of the American presidents between 1945 and 1996, while the red-and-white areas flash clips from the news.

👁 Can you find the one other American flag in this wing?

NEO-EXPRESSIONISM
Paint What's Inside

The Neo-Expressionists were the new ("neo") generation of Expressionist painters. They were inspired by the bold colors and textured brushstrokes of earlier modern art styles, such as German Expressionism (see room 96). They didn't make art that forced people to think too hard to understand it, like Conceptual art (see room 110). They wanted to paint people, places, and things to show how they felt about the world around them.

WEARING THE CROWN
JEAN-MICHEL BASQUIAT, GRILLO, 1984

Jean-Michel Basquiat first started creating art by spraying graffiti onto trains and buildings with his friends. Artists and critics took notice of his work, and eventually, he started making art to show in galleries. Basquiat is famous for his energetic paintings. The lively emotions come through the scratchy lines, written words, and bold colors. Do you spy the crowns in this painting?

Many of Basquiat's paintings show Black figures wearing crowns or halos to celebrate them as heroes and royalty. The spiky crown on the figure to the left is similar to the Nkisi sculptures from Central Africa. Nkisi sculptures have sharp pieces of metal sticking out of them, so Basquiat hammered real nails into some parts of this artwork.

CONTEMPORARY PAINTING
Happening Now

ROOM 128

In art history, the contemporary era begins in the 1960s and goes up to the present day. It includes all of the different **movements** that you have discovered in this gallery. Some styles don't even have names yet because they are still being developed by artists working today. In the future, historians may look back and group these ideas into new movements. This final room displays a selection of paintings from the 1980s to the 2000s.

HONEST PORTRAITS
ALICE NEEL, SELF-PORTRAIT, 1980

This is one of only two self-portraits Alice Neel ever made, and it took five years to finish. It shows Neel when she was 80 years old, and she has painted her body exactly as it looked. She joked that her cheeks are red because the painting took such so much time and effort to do! Many of the figures in Alice Neel's artworks appear to make eye contact with the viewer. It creates a greater emotional connection between the person who's looking and the artwork.

👁 Can you find another self-portrait in wing two that shows the artist holding a paintbrush?

CLOSE-UP CURIOSITY
YOSHITOMO NARA, I WANT TO SEE THE BRIGHT LIGHTS TONIGHT, 2017

Yoshitomo Nara has a unique style that's easy to spot. Many of his paintings show a close-up view of a child against a solid color background. The figures usually have simple features, like large eyes and a straight line for a mouth. What do you think the girl in this painting is thinking? Nara likes to paint a person who expresses feelings, like sadness or rebelliousness, and lets you imagine a story around them.

👁 Nara's works are sometime compared to cartoons. Can you find another cartoonlike image on p.196?

216 The Ultimate Art Museum

LUNCH ON THE GRASS

KERRY JAMES MARSHALL, PAST TIMES, 1997

Past Times is one of Kerry James Marshall's great masterpieces. It shows a Black family enjoying a sunny picnic by a lake. If it wasn't for the modern features, like the speedboat and skyscrapers in the background, this could look like it was made in the time of Édouard Manet's paintings (see p.163). That was the intention! Marshall paints Black figures in the grand styles from the Renaissance to the present in order to celebrate them in a way that they were not shown across the history of Western art.

THE FIRST LADY

AMY SHERALD, FIRST LADY MICHELLE OBAMA, 2018

This is a portrait of Michelle Obama, who is married to the 44th president of the US, Barack Obama. Each president and his wife (the First Lady) have their portraits painted toward the end of their time in office. Amy Sherald's paintings of people are usually colorful everywhere except for the person's skin. The skin is painted to look like a black-and-white photograph. She's inspired by old photographs and how, in the past, Black families used cameras to photograph their lives in the way they wanted to show themselves.

? ART DETECTIVE

Michelle Obama's dress in this painting is inspired by the bold quilt designs of a group of Black women from Gee's Bend, Alabama. These women and their ancestors have been making quilts since the early 1800s, even when the early members of the community were enslaved on a plantation owned by Joseph Gee.

Postmodern and Contemporary Art Since the Mid-20th Century

HALL OF SELFIES

Why not stop for a selfie to share your visit with friends? Before you whip out your phone or dip that paintbrush, take in some arty inspiration. Artists have been making selfies for centuries!

SHOW HOW YOU FEEL INSIDE

FRIDA KAHLO, THE TWO FRIDAS, 1939

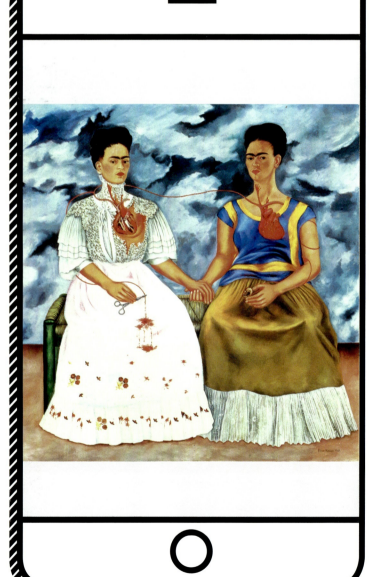

Frida Kahlo's painting shows two portraits with her heart on her chest. One heart is broken.

PUT ON YOUR BEST SMILE

YUE MINJUN, CONTEMPORARY TERRACOTTA WARRIOR, 2000

Yue Minjun's selfies show him with a giant smile. They make you wonder, what's so funny?

218 The Ultimate Art Museum

DRESS TO IMPRESS!
CINDY SHERMAN, UNTITLED FILM STILL #58, 1980

Cindy Sherman photographs herself wearing lots of costumes. You can dress up how you like in a selfie!

STRIKE A POSE WITH THE ONE YOU LOVE
GLUCK, MEDALLION (YOUWE), 1936

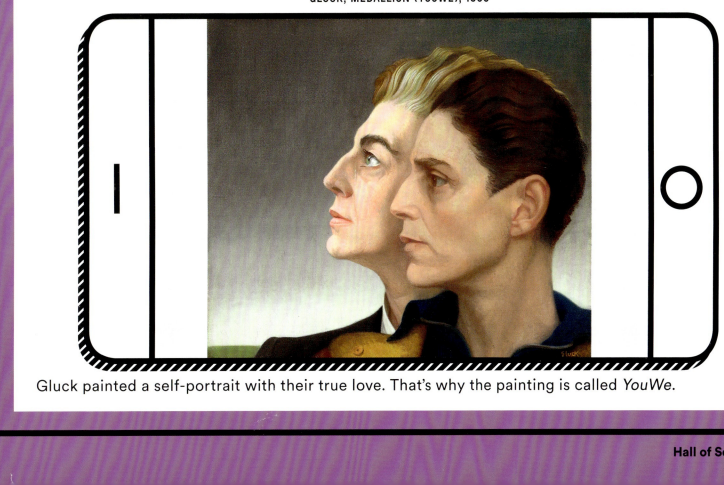

Gluck painted a self-portrait with their true love. That's why the painting is called *YouWe*.

A MESSAGE FROM YOUR ART HISTORIAN

When I was in school, history was one of my favorite subjects! I loved to hear stories about places around the world, and it seemed to me that history lessons had all the ingredients for a perfect tale. They included epic battles, love stories, and long journeys. But unlike fairy tales, all of it really happened. When I learned about art history, I was overjoyed to discover that I could dive in and out of history by looking at paintings, objects, and architecture. Suddenly, my favorite stories had pictures!

People sometimes ask me what sort of jobs they can do if they study art history. I'm happy to tell you that the opportunities are endless! You could work on a film set giving advice about making scenes look historically accurate or work with the police to track down sneaky art thieves. Art historians can travel the world to dig up ancient ruins or even pick up a paintbrush to carefully restore fading masterpieces.

If you have been excited by the artworks within this museum, I encourage you to visit as many museums as you can. It feels incredible to sit in front of a beautiful painting for the first time! If you were inspired by a particular artist or section, ask your parents if they can help you find more information. There are entire galleries, books, and websites dedicated to individual artists. By exploring this museum, you're already well on your way to becoming an amazing art historian. Maybe one day, you can create a museum of your own...

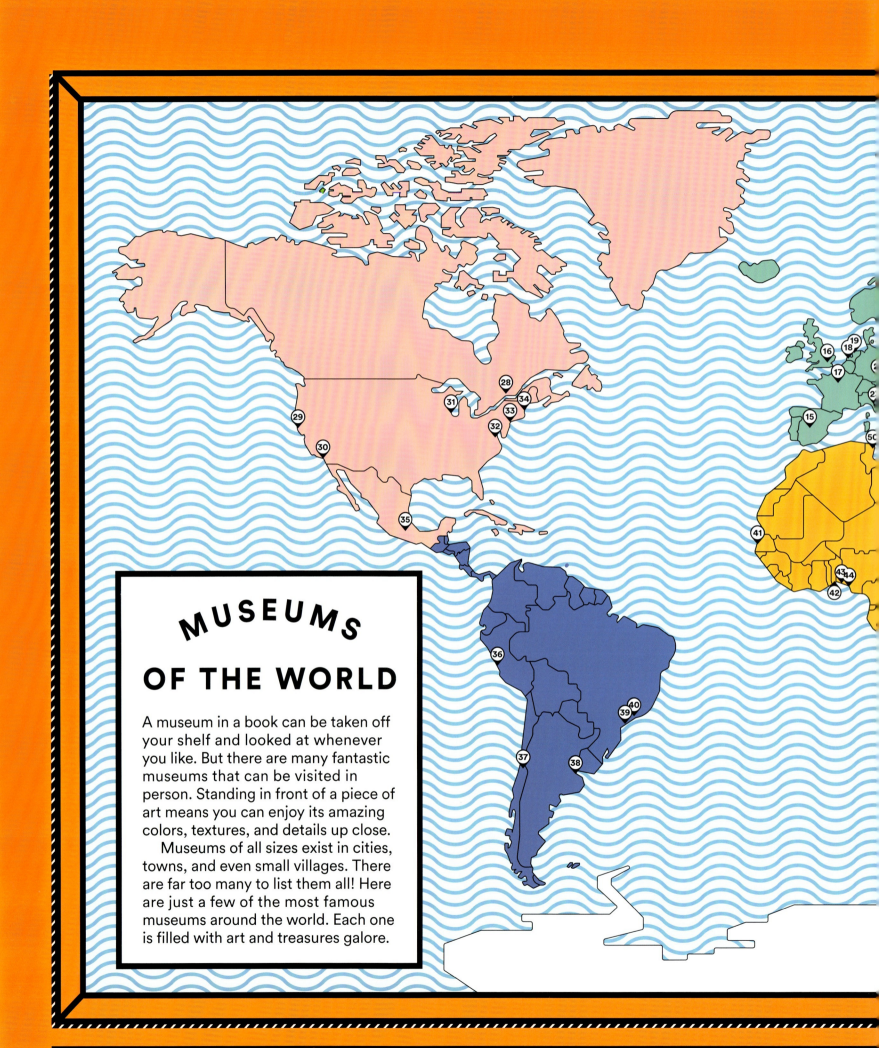

MUSEUMS OF THE WORLD

A museum in a book can be taken off your shelf and looked at whenever you like. But there are many fantastic museums that can be visited in person. Standing in front of a piece of art means you can enjoy its amazing colors, textures, and details up close.

Museums of all sizes exist in cities, towns, and even small villages. There are far too many to list them all! Here are just a few of the most famous museums around the world. Each one is filled with art and treasures galore.

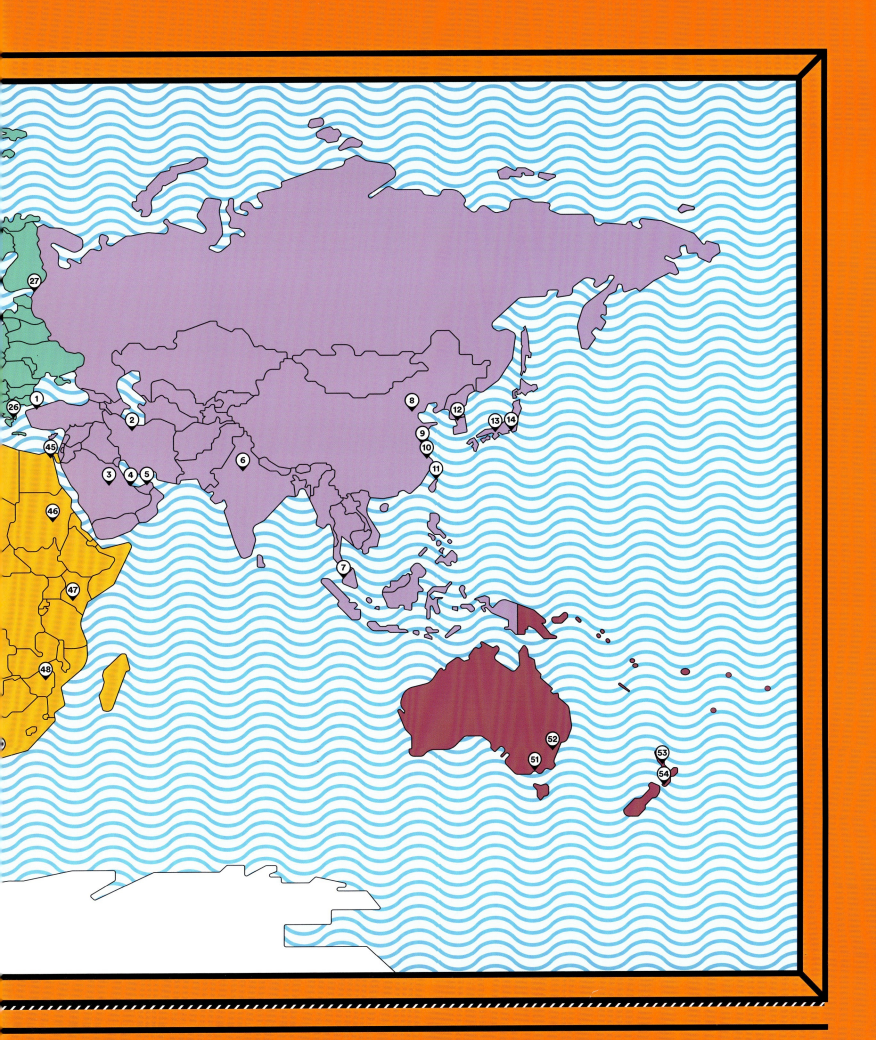

Museums of the World 223

MUSEUMS OF THE WORLD

ASIA
1. Istanbul, Turkey: Topkapi Palace Museum
2. Tehran, Iran: Tehran Museum of Contemporary Art
3. Riyadh, Saudi Arabia: National Museum of Saudi Arabia
4. Doha, Qatar:
   - Museum of Islamic Art
   - Arab Museum of Modern Art
5. Sharjah, United Arab Emirates: The Sharjah Art Museum
6. New Delhi, India:
   - National Gallery of Modern Art
   - National Museum
7. Kuala Lumpur, Malaysia: Islamic Arts Museum Malaysia
8. Beijing, China: National Museum of China
9. Nanjing, China: Nanjing Museum
10. Hangzhou, China: Zhejiang Museum
11. Taipei, Taiwan: National Palace Museum
12. Seoul, South Korea: National Museum of Korea
13. Kyoto, Japan: Kyoto National Museum
14. Tokyo, Japan: Tokyo National Museum

EUROPE
15. Madrid, Spain
    - Reina Sofia
    - Museo Nacional del Prado
16. London, United Kingdom:
    - British Museum
    - Tate
    - National Gallery
    - Victoria and Albert Museum
17. Paris, France:
    - Musée du Louvre
    - Musée d'Orsay
18. The Hague, Netherlands: Mauritshuis
19. Amsterdam, Netherlands: Rijksmuseum
20. Berlin, Germany:
    - Pergamon Museum
    - Neues Museum
21. Munich, Germany: Alte Pinakothek
22. Vienna, Austria: Kunsthistorisches Museum
23. Florence, Italy: Uffizi Gallery
24. Vatican City, Italy: Vatican Museums
25. Naples, Italy: Museo Archeologico Nazionale di Napoli
26. Athens, Greece:
    - National Archaeological Museum
    - Acropolis Museum
27. St Petersburg, Russia: State Hermitage Museum

NORTH AMERICA
28. Ottawa, Canada: National Gallery of Canada

29. San Francisco, USA: San Francisco Museum of Modern Art
30. Los Angeles, USA: Los Angeles County Museum of Art
31. Chicago, USA: Art Institute of Chicago
32. Washington D.C., USA:
    - National Gallery of Art
    - National Museum of African American History and Culture
33. New York, USA:
    - The Metropolitan Museum of Art
    - Museum of Modern Art
34. Boston, USA: Museum of Fine Arts
35. Mexico City, Mexico:
    - Museo Nacional de Arte
    - Museo de Arte Moderno

CENTRAL AND SOUTH AMERICA

36. Lima, Peru: Museo de Arte de Lima
37. Santiago, Chile: Museo Nacional de Bellas Artes
38. Buenos Aires, Argentina:
    - Museo Nacional de Bellas Artes
    - Museo de Arte Latinoamericano de Buenos Aires
39. Sao Paulo, Brazil: Museu de Arte de São Paulo
40. Rio de Janiero, Brazil: Museu de Arte Moderna do Rio de Janeiro

AFRICA

41. Dakar, Senegal: Museum of Black Civilization
42. Cotonou, Benin: Fondation Zinsou
43. Lagos, Nigeria: Nigerian National Museum
44. Lekki, Nigeria: Yemisi Shyllon Museum of Art
45. Cairo, Egypt: The Egyptian Museum
46. Khartoum, Sudan: Sudan National Museum
47. Nairobi, Kenya: Nairobi National Museum
48. Harare, Zimbabwe: National Gallery of Zimbabwe
49. Cape Town, South Africa:
    - Zeitz Museum of Contemporary Art Africa
    - Iziko South African National Gallery
50. Tunis, Tunisia: Bardo Museum

AUSTRALASIA

51. Melbourne, Australia: National Gallery of Victoria
52. Canberra, Australia: National Gallery of Australia
53. Auckland, New Zealand: Auckland Art Gallery Toi o Tāmaki
54. Wellington, New Zealand: Museum of New Zealand Te Papa Tongarewa

GLOSSARY

Abstract: not showing people or things in a realistic way; abstract art can show recognizable pictures or nothing in particular.

Analytical Cubism: a style of art in which the artist has analyzed an object in detail and experimented with how to show its entire three-dimensional shape on a flat surface.

Architecture: the art of making buildings.

Art academies: schools where artists train in painting, drawing, sculpture, and other fine art skills.

Artisans: people who use special skills to make things with their hands, like making silk.

Bronze: a metal made by combining the two metals copper and tin.

Busts: sculptures or casts of the upper part of the body, including the head, neck, and shoulders.

Ceramic: clay that has been shaped and heated at a very high temperature to become hard.

Chiaroscuro: Italian word meaning "light" (*chiaro*) and "dark" (*scuro*). In art, it refers to strong differences in bright and shaded areas.

Classical art: artworks that were made or influenced by the cultures of ancient Greece and Rome.

Contrast: a strong difference between two elements of an artwork, such as light and dark or hard and soft.

Darkroom: a room with very little light (often a red light) that is used for developing or making photographs.

Diptych: any artwork made of two pieces or parts that is meant to be viewed as one work.

Embroidered: fabric or other materials that have been decorated with designs sewn on with a needle and thread.

Experimental: a new and inventive style of art or technique.

Figurines: small carved statues, often in the shape of people or animals.

Form: the shape of a person or thing.

Fresco: a painting made on a wall while the plaster is wet (also called *buon fresco*). When paints that are mixed with special materials go on dry plaster, it's called fresco-secco.

Geometric: an image or pattern made from shapes or lines.

Idealized: a way of representing somebody or something as being perfect or better than they really are.

Impasto: a type of oil painting in which the paint is applied in very thick layers.

Installation: an artwork (often a large one) that has been specially designed to change the way people experience a place.

Mosaic: patterns or pictures made with small pieces of cut stone, ceramic, or glass, or with pebbles.

Movement: a style of art by a group of artists whose artworks share similar looks, ideas, or inspirations, such as the Abstract Expressionist movement.

Myths: stories, especially ones from ancient times, that helps explain parts of nature or the early history of a culture.

Negative space: the empty or open space around an object in a painting or sculpture.

Non-representational: an image that does not show a recognizable person, place, or thing.

Perspective: creating an effect of distance or depth in art so that it appears more three-dimensional, such as showing things that are far away as being smaller than those that are nearer the front.

Photomontage: a picture that is made up of different photographs put together; the technique of making these pictures.

Pigments: colored materials that can be mixed with a liquid, such as water or oil, to make paint.

Pointillism: a painting technique that involves using small, painted dots to create areas of color that come together to form a picture or pattern.

Printmaker: an artist who prints pictures or designs.

Relic: an object that once belonged to a holy person and that is kept after their death as a respected religious item.

Sculpture: a three-dimensional artwork made by carving, molding, or assembling materials, such as wood, stone, clay, metal, and even pre-made objects.

Silk: a natural thread made mostly by silkworms. It can be woven into a very soft and smooth fabric.

Stencils: thin materials, such as a pieces of paper or plastic, with designs cut out of them that can be traced or painted to put a picture on another surface.

Still life: pictures of objects, such as flowers, food, and dishes.

Symbolism: the use of pictures or objects to represent ideas.

Tapestry: a heavy cloth that has designs or pictures woven into it. It can be used as a wall hanging.

Temple: a building that is used for worship.

Textiles: cloth or woven materials, such as clothes, rugs, tapestries, blankets, and fabric.

Three-dimensional: an object or shape that has three dimensions—length, width, and height.

Two-dimensional: a flat shape or figure that has two dimensions—length and width.

Volcanic glass: a natural glass produced when molten lava from a volcano cools very quickly.

Wax print: a popular fabric in West African cultures with colorful designs that can hold special meanings for different groups of people; also called African wax prints or Dutch wax prints.

Western: in art history, a term generally used to refer to cultures from North America and Europe.

INDEX

Page numbers in *italics* refer to illustrations

A
Aboriginal Australian art 207, *207*
abstract art 36, *36*, 184, 188
Abstract Expressionism 188–89
Actaeon 126, *126*
African art 146–53, 158
   masks 168, *168*, 169
Akbar 104, *104*
Akkad, King of 20, *20*
Aksumite empire 151
Albers, Anni 202, *202*
altarpieces 124–25
Alÿs, Francis 213, *213*
Ambrym 145
American realism 167
American regionalism 174, 175
Amphitrite 41, *41*
Analytical Cubism 169
Ancient Near-East 18–87
Andrew, Saint 66, *66*
Anglo-Saxons 62, 64
Anubis 28, *28*
Aphrodite 41, *41*
architecture 42, 56, 69
Arcimboldo, Giuseppe 97, *97*
Ardabil Carpet 115, *115*
Ashoka, Emperor 84
Ashurnasirpal II, King 21, *21*
Asia, arts of 100–115
Assyrian Empire 21, 22
Augustus Caesar 45, *45*
Aydakin ibn 'abd Allah 61
Azana, King 151
Aztecs 88, 92, 94, *94*, 181

B
Babylonian Empire 22, 24
Bamana culture 149
bamboo 107, *107*
Bamum people 150, *150*
Baroque style 130–31, 132
Basquiat, Jean-Michel 215
Bastet 33
Bauhaus 202
Bayeux Tapestry 68, *68*
Bearden, Romare 185, *185*
Bellows, George 167, *167*
Bengal School 180
Benin people 148, *148*
Bhairava 86, *86*
Bible, the 54, *54*, 69, 151, 177, *177*
Black American narratives 176–77
Blombos Caves 152
Der Blaue Reiter 172, 173
Boccioni, Umberto 170, *170*
Bodhisattva 87, *87*
Bonheur, Rosa 141, *141*
Book of Hours 69, *69*
Book of Kells 59, 67, *67*
Borobudur panel 86, *86*
Bosch, Hieronymus 124, *124*
Botticelli, Sandro 118, *118*, 121, 166
Bourgeois, Louise 201, *201*
Braque, Georges 169, *169*
Breton, André 182
Bronze Age 37
Bronze Age, Chinese 72
Die Brüke 172, 173
Bruegel, Pieter the Elder 127, *127*
buckles 64, *64*
Buddha 78, *78*, 81, *81*, 82, 84, 87
Buddhism 70, 78, *78*, 81, 82, 84, 86, 103
Burkina Faso 149, 168
busts 45, 49, 176, *176*
Bwa people 168, *168*
Byzantine art 50–55, 68, 151

C
Calder, Alexander 201, *201*
calligraphy 60
Caravaggio, Michelangelo Merisi da 130, *130*
carpet designs 115, *115*
Carriera, Rosalba 134, *134*
carvings 145, *145*
Cassatt, Mary 163, *163*
Catholic Church 116, 130
cats 33, *33*
cattle 16, 32, *32*
cave paintings 14–16
Celmins, Vija 211, *211*
Central Africa 150
ceramics 74, *74*, 79, *79*, 91, 111, *111*
Cézanne, Paul 96, *96*, 169
chariot model 24, *24*
Chartres Cathedral 69, *69*
chiaroscuro 131
Chicago, Judy 208, *208*
Chicanx art 209
China 70, 72–76, 78, 79, 106–9, 111
chocolate 93
Chŏng Sŏn 110, *110*
Christianity 50, 52, 53, 54, 62, 66, 68, 130, 151
Christo and Jeanne-Claude 206, *206*
Claudius 45, *45*
collage 185, *185*, 210
color field 190–91
columns 48, *48*
Conceptual art 194, 213, 215
cong tube 73, *73*
Constable, John 138, *138*
Constantine the Great 50
Contemporary art 186–219
cosmetics box lid 23, *23*
Courbet, Gustave 141, *141*
cowrie shells 150
Coyolxauhqui 94, *94*
crosses, processional 151, *151*
Cubism 169, 170, 185, 189, 193
Cueva de las Manos 16, *16*
Cupid 45, 131
cups 37, *37*
Cycladic Bronze Age art 36
Cyrus II, King 24

D
Dada 171, 182, 185, 198
daggers 37, *37*
Dai, Lady 74, *74*
Dalí, Salvador 183, *183*
Daoism 111
David 119, *119*, 121, *121*
David, Jacques-Louis 136, 137, *137*
David vases 111, *111*
de Kooning, Willem 189, *189*
De Morgan, Evelyn 166, *166*
De Stijl 178, 179
decolonizing art 212
decorative arts 105, *105*
Degas, Edgar 163, *163*
Delilah 131, *131*
Diana 126, *126*
ding bronzes 72, *72*
Dinwoody cultures 90, *90*
Dionysos 39, *39*
diptychs 55, *55*
Doesburg, Theo van 179
Dogon culture 148, 149
dogū 80
Donatello 119, *119*, 121
Dong Qichang 106, *106*
Duchamp, Marcel 170, *170*, 171, *171*, 201
Duncanson, Robert 138, *138*
dupun 207, *207*
Dürer, Albrecht 123, *123*
Dutch Golden Age 132–33
Dynamic Cubism 177

E
eagle warriors 94, *94*
East Africa 153
East Asia 70–81
Egyptians, ancient 26–33, 40
Ethiopian Christian art 151
Etruscans 42–44
European painting 128–41
European Realism 141, 163

European Renaissance 116–27
Expressionism 172–73, 188, 215
Eyck, Hubert van 125, *125*
Eyck, Jan van 116, 122, *122*, 125, *125*, 136

F
Faith, Saint 66, *66*
fang hu 72, *72*
Fauvism 165, 172
feminist art 208
fêtes galantes 135
figurative art 146, 153
figurines 17, *17*, 36, *36*, 80, *80*
fish vessel 33, *33*
fisherman 36, *36*
Flavin, Dan 203, *203*
Fontana, Lavinia 121, *121*
Four Gentlemen, the 107
Fragonard, Jean-Honoré 135, *135*
Frankenthaler, Helen *190–91*, 191
frescos 36, *36*, 44, *44*, 46, *46*, 86, 87, *87*
Fuji, Mount 160, *160*
Futurism 170

G
Gabriel 55, *55*
Gainsborough, Thomas 134, *134*
Ganesha 85
Garza, Carmen Lomas 209, *209*
Gayer-Anderson cat 33, *33*
Gee, Joseph 217
Genji, Hikaru 113, *113*
genre painting 127, 132, 133
Gentileschi, Artemisia 131, *131*, 208
Geometric Period 38
George, Saint 118, *118*
Géricault, Théodore 140, *140*
German Expressionism 172, 173, 215
Ghent Altarpiece 125, *125*
Gluck 219, *219*
gods and goddesses 28
Gogh, Van Vincent 164, *164*, 172, 191
Gothic art 62, 69, 122
Great Depression 174, 175
Great Migration 176
Great Stupa, Sanchi 84, *84*
Greeks, ancient 34–41, 49, 121, 136
griffin rhyton 24, *24*
Grimms' Fairy Tales 140
Guan Daosheng 107, *107*
Gwandusu 149, *149*

H
Hades 39, *39*
Hafiz 115

Hall of the Bulls, Lascaux *14–15*, 15
Hamilton, Richard 197, *197*
Haniwa 80, *80*
Harlem Renaissance 177
hazomanga 153
headrests 152, *152*
Heggen vane 65, *65*
Hehe people 153, *153*
Hellenistic period 40
helmets 64, *64*
Hemessen, Catharina van 123, *123*
Hepworth, Barbara 184, *184*
Hernandez, Ester 209, *209*
High Italian Renaissance 120–21
Hinduism 82, 85, 86
hippopotamus 33, *33*
Hiroshige, Utagawa 161, *161*
Hirschfeld krater 38, *38*
Hirst, Damien 194, *194*
history paintings 126, *126*
Höch, Hannah 185, *185*
Hockney, David 197, *197*
Hokusai, Katsushika 160, *160*, 210
Holbein, Hans the Younger 122, *122*
Holzer, Jenny 203, *203*
Hongshan culture 73
Hopewell peoples 91, *91*
Hopper, Edward 167, *167*
Hudson River School 138
Huitzilopochtli 94
Huizong, Emperor 76, *76*

I
ibn al-Zayn, Muhammad 60, *60*
ibol 150, *150*
icons 53, *53*
Ife 148
illuminated manuscripts 54, *54*, 67, *67*, 151, *151*
impasto 164, *164*
Impressionism 139, 162–63, 164, 203
Inca Empire 88, 92, 95, *95*
incense burners 79, *79*
Indian modernism 180
Indiana, Robert 197, *197*
Ingres, Jean-Auguste-Dominique 136, *136*
installation art 199, 205
Iranian art 23
Ishtar Gate 22, *22*
Islamic art 56–61
  carpet designs 115, *115*
Italian Renaissance 120–21
ivory 55, 85, 148, *148*

J
jade 73, *73*
janiform aryballos 38, *38*

Japan 80–81
  Japanese art 158, 160–61
  Japanese screens 112, *112*
Jesus Christ 55, 67, 69, *69*, 151, *151*
  Christ Pantokrator 53, *53*
Johnson, William H. 176, *176*
Jōmon 80
Justinian I 52, *52*

K
Kahlo, Frida 218, *218*
Kandinsky, Wassily 173, *173*
Kang Hŭian 110, *110*
Kangxi Emperor *108–9*, 109
Kapoor, Anish 200, *200*
Kashani, Maqsud 115, *115*
Kauffman, Angelica 137, *137*
Kelly, Ellsworth 193, *193*
Kencana Wungu 105, *105*
kinetic sculptures 201
Kirchner, Ernst Ludwig 172, *172*
Kitano Shinto shrine 81, *81*
Klimt, Gustav 155, *155*
Kollwitz, Käthe 173, *173*
Korean art 77, 78–79, 110, 111, *111*
kouros 184, *184*
Krasner, Lee 188, *188*, 189
Kroisos 40, *40*
Kuba kingdom 150, 168
Kufic 60
Kusama, Yayoi *204–205*, 205
Kûya 81, *81*

L
Lalibela 151
lamps, mosque 61, *61*
land art 206
Lange, Dorothea 175, *175*
Laocoön 41, *41*
Lascaux caves *14–15*, 15
Lawrence, Jacob 177, *177*
Leonardo da Vinci 116, 120, *120*, 121, 202
Levantine art 23
LeWitt, Sol 194, *194*
Leyster, Judith 133, *133*
Lichtenstein, Roy 196, *196*
light 203–205
lintels, carved 144, *144*
Lion Man of Hohlenstein-Stadel 17, *17*
Liwangu, Johnny 207, *207*
Louis XIV, King 134

M
Maar, Dora 182
Madagascar 153

Magritte, René 182, *182*
Malevich, Kazimir 178, *178*
Mali 149
mana 144
Manchus 109
Manet, Édouard 163, *163*, 217
manuscripts, illuminated 54, *54*, 67, *67*
Marie Antoinette, Queen 136, *136*
Marshall, Kerry James 217, *217*
masks 145, *145*, 148, *148*, 150, *150*, 158, 168, *168*, 169
Matisse, Henri 165, *165*, 168
Matthew, Saint 67, *67*
Maya 88, 91, 93, *93*, 181
Medici family 121
Medieval Europe 62–69
Medusa 140, *140*
Meketre 32
Melanesia 145, *145*
Merian, Maria Sibylla 154, *154*
Mesopotamian art 18–25
Mexican muralism 181
Michael, Archangel 53, *53*
Michelangelo 41, 120, 121, *121*
Michizane, Sugawara no 81
Micronesia 144
mihrab 59, *59*
Millais, John Everett 166, *166*
Mimbres culture 90, *90*
mimi 207
miniature painting 102–3, 180
Minimalism 192–93, 203
Minoan art 37
Mississippian cultures 91
Mitchell, Joan 188, *188*
Mithras 23, *23*
Mitsuyoshi, Tosa 113
moai 144, *144*
Modern Art 158–85
modernism, Indian 180
Mondrian, Piet 179, *179*
Monet, Claude 162, *162*
Mongol Empire 100, 106, 107
Morisot, Berthe 162, *162*
mosaics 34, 39, 47, *47*, 52, *52*, 58, *58*
mosques 59, *59*, 61
Mughal architecture, 114
Mughal Empire 100, 103, 104, 115, 180
Muhammad, Prophet 56, 59
mummies 26, 28, 30
Munch, Edvard 172, *172*
muralism, Mexican 181
Mycenaean art 37
mythical art 39

N
Napoleon I 136, 137
Nara, Yoshitomo 216, *216*
narrative art 65, *65*
Naskh 60
native cultures 88–95
n'dop 150, *150*
Nebamum 29, *29*
Neel, Alice 216, *216*
Nefertiti 30, *30*
negative space 184
Neo-Classical 136–37, 140
Neo-Expressionism 215, *215*
Neshat, Shirin 210, *210*
Nevelson, Louise 200, *200*
Ngaady-A-Mwaash 168, *168*
Nguni people 152, *152*
Nike of Samothrace 40, *40*
Nile, River 32, 33
Noguchi, Isamu 184, *184*
nomads 23
non-representational art 188, 189
North American native cultures 88–95
Northern Renaissance 122–25
Nubian archers 32, *32*
Nyim Mishé miShyááng máMbúl 150, *150*

O
Obama, Michelle 217
O'Keeffe, Georgia 154, *154*, 208
Oldenburg, Claes 97, *97*
Olmecs 88, 92, 181
oni 148, *148*
Op art 195
Oppenheim, Meret 182, *182*
Orozco, José Clemente 181, *181*

P
Pacific art 142–45
Paik, Nam June 214, *214*
Pakal I, K'inich Janaab' 93, *93*
palepai 105, *105*
Paris Gregory 54, *54*
Parks, Gordon 175, *175*
Peeters, Clara 97, *97*
performance art 213, 214
Persephone 39, *39*
Persepolis reliefs 25, *25*
Persian Empire 24–25
petroglyphs 90, *90*
pets 33, *33*
pharaohs 29, 30
photography 158, 175, 210, 211
photomontage 185, *185*
Picasso, Pablo 168, 169, *169*, 182, 189, 202
pig-dragons 73, *73*
pointillism 164, *164*

Pollock, Jackson 189, *189*
Polynesia 144
Pompeii 46, *46*, 137
Pop art 196–97
Post-Impressionism 164
Postmodernism 186–219
pottery
  Chinese and Korean 79, *79*, 111, *111*
  Greek 38
  Inca 95, *95*
Pottery Wars (1592–1597) 111
Powers, Harriet 177, *177*
Pre-Raphaelites 166
prehistoric art 12–17
Prometheus 181
punch'ŏng 111, *111*
puppets 105, *105*

Q
Qin Shi Huangdi 75, *75*
quattrocento 118–19, 166
quilts 177, *177*
Qur'an 56, 59, 61, *61*, 114

R
Rama 102–3, *103*
Ramayana 87, 102–3, 103
Ramingining 207
Rapa Nui (Easter Island) 144, *144*
Raphael 120, *120*, 121, 166
Rauschenberg, Robert 198, *198*
Ray, Man 171, *171*
readymade sculpture 171, *171*
Realism 141, 163
  American realism 167
red-figure pottery 38, *38*
relics 66, *66*
reliefs 21, *21*, 25, *25*, 31, 55, *55*, 69, *69*, 86, 119, *119*
reliquaries 66, *66*
Rembrandt van Rijn 133, *133*
Renaissance 115, 116–27, 166
Riace warriors 40, *40*
Richter, Gerhard 211, *211*
Riley, Bridget 195, *195*
Ringgold, Faith 202, *202*
Rist, Pipilotti 214, *214*
Rivera, Diego 181, *181*
rock paintings 14–16
Rococo 134–35
rom masks 145, *145*
Romanesque style 68, 69
Romans 34, 42–49, 50, 66, 68, 136
Romanticism 140
Rossi, Properzia de' 119, *119*
Rothko, Mark 192, *192*
Rousseau, Henri 155, *155*

Ru ware 79, *79*
Rubens, Peter Paul 131, *131*
Ruysch, Rachel 132, *132*

S
Saar, Betye 198, *198*
Safi al-Din Ardabili 115
Sakalava 153, *153*
Sakhmet 28, *28*
Samson 131, *131*
Sancho, Ignatius 134, *134*
Sarpedon 38, *38*
Savage, Augusta 176, *176*, 177
Schapiro, Miriam 208, *208*
scholar-officials 106
scholar paintings 110, *110*
sculpture: African 148–50
   Buddhist 78, *78*
   Chinese 74, *74*
   Gothic 69, *69*
   Greek 40–41, 49
   Hindu 85, *85*, 86
   Japanese 80, *80*
   Mississippian culture 91, *91*
   modern and contemporary 184, 198, 199, 200, 201
   relief 55, *55*
   Roman 49, *49*
selfies 218–19
Seurat, Georges 164, *164*
Shahibdin 103
Sher-Gil, Amrita 180, *180*
Sherald, Amy 217, *217*
Sherman, Cindy 219, *219*
shields 145, *145*
Shikibu, Murasaki 113, *113*
Shintō 81
Shiva, Lord 85, *85*, 86
Shonibare, Yinka 212, *212*
shrines 81, *81*
Siddal, Elizabeth 166
silk paintings 74, *74*, 76, *76*
Silk Road 100
Sirani, Elisabetta 130, *130*
Smith, David 201, *201*
Soto, Jesús Rafael 195, *195*
South and Southeast Asia 82–87
Southern Africa 152
spearthrowers 17, *17*
Standard of Ur 20, *20*
Stella, Frank 193
Stephen, Saint 68, *68*
stereotypes 167
still life 132
Stone Age 12–17
stonework 86–87
Stora Hammars Stone 65, *65*

stupa 84, *84*
Sumerian votive statuette 20, *20*
Suprematism 178
Surrealism 182–83
Sutton Hoo 64

T
Tagore, Abanindranath 180, *180*
Taj Mahal, 114, *114*
The Tale of Genji 113, *113*
Tane 144, *144*
Tanner, Henry Ossawa 167, *167*
Tanning, Dorothea 183, *183*
Tan'yū, Kanō 112, *112*
Tanzania 153
tapestries 68, *68*
Tassel Bradshaw painting 16, *16*
temple art 86
Terracotta Warriors 75, *75*
textiles 76, *76*, 202
Tguni people 152
Thera ship fresco 36, *36*
Thiebaud, Wayne 97, *97*
Thomas, Alma 192, *192*
3D art 200–201
thrones 153, *153*
Thutmose III 31, *31*
Titian 126, *126*
tocapu 95, *95*
Tōhaku, Hasegawa 112, *112*
tomb art 70, 74, *74*, 75, *75*, 77, *77*, 80, *80*
Tomb of the Leopards 44, *44*
Tosa school 113
Trajan's Column 48, *48*
Truth, Sojourner 208
Tsonga people 152, *152*
Tubman, Harriet 176, *176*, 177, *177*
Turner, J. M. W 138, 139, *139*
Tutankhamun 30, *30*
Twyfelfontein 16, *16*

U
Uccello, Paolo 118, *118*
ukiyo-e 160, *160*, 163
ultra-realistic paintings 211
Umayyads 58
unusual materials 198
urpu 95, *95*

V
Valkryies 65
vapheio cup 37, *37*
Vasari, Giorgio 119
vases 23, *23*, 38, *38*
Velázquez, Diego 130, *130*
vellum 54
Venus 49, *49*, 131

Venus de Milo 41, *41*
Venus of Willendorf 17, *17*
Vermeer, Johannes 132, *132*
Vesuvius, Mount 46, 137
vicuña wool 95, *95*
video art 214, *214*
Vigée Le Brun, Élisabeth Louise 136, *136*
Vikings 62, 65
Virgin Mary 55, *55*
Vishnu 85, *85*, 103

W
Walker, Kara 212, *212*
Wall, Jeff 210, *210*
Wang Hui 108–9, 109
Warhol, Andy 196, *196*, 197
Watteau, Jean-Antoine 135, *135*
wayang golek puppet 105, *105*
West Africa 148–49
Whistler, James McNeill 161, *161*
Whiteread, Rachel 199, *199*
William of Ockham 203
wishbone-handled cup 37, *37*
Wood, Grant 174, *174*, 175
woodblock prints 160, *160*, *161*, 173
Woodland cultures 91, *91*
Wright of Derby, Joseph 137, *137*
writing 60

X
Xu Bing 199, *199*

Y
yamato-e images 112, *112*
Yoruba culture 148, *148*
Yue Minjun 218, *218*

Z
zebu vase 23, *23*
Zhao Mengfu 107, *107*

PICTURE CREDITS

We would like to thank all those who gave their permission to reproduce the listed material. Every effort has been made to secure all permissions prior to publication. Phaidon apologizes for any inadvertent errors or omissions. If notified, the publisher will endeavour to correct these at the earliest opportunity.

All works in copyright are © the artists or their estates

© ADAGP, Paris and DACS, London 2021: 169l; akg-images / Album: 119r, 138t / Bildarchiv Monheim: 69l, / The de Morgan Foundation, London: 166l, / Heritage Images / Fine Art Images: 155b, / Erich Lessing: 36bl, 97tr, 97bl, 132r, 161r, / MONDADORI PORTFOLIO / Luciano Pedicini / Reproduced with permission of Ministero per i Beni e le Attività Culturali: 130bl, / Pictures from History: 107r, / Science Source: 39bl, 39br; Alamy Stock Photo: / © A.P: 65l, / © Bildarchiv Monheim GmbH: 59l, Danita Delimont Creative: 114, / The History Collection: 107l, / imageBROKER / Photo: Raimund Kutter: 44, / © Neil McAllister: 86t, / Niday Picture Library: 180l; © ARS, NY and DACS, London 2021: 194b; © the artist: 184r; Courtesy of the Artist: 209r; © the artist: 210b; © the artist: 213; © the artist: 216l; © the artist/Art Gallery of Ontario, Toronto, Canada: 97tl; © the artist / Hirshhorn Museum and Sculpture Garden, Smithsonian Institution: 214b; © the artist / Image courtesy the artist and Stephen Friedman Gallery (London) and James Cohan Gallery (New York) / Vanhaerents Art Collection, Brussels, Belgium / © Yinka Shonibare CBE. All Rights Reserved, DACS 2021: 212t; © the artists/Photographer: Harry Shunk / © ADAGP, Paris and DACS, London 2021: 206; © the artist / Courtesy Yayoi Kusama Studio / Victoria Miro Gallery, London and Ota Fine Arts, Tokyo / Photography by Norihiro Ueno: 204-205; © Asian Art Museum of San Francisco / The Avery Brundage Collection: 112t, 113r; © Photograph 1985 Dirk Bakker: 91l; Bayerische Staatsgemäldesammlungen – Alte Pinakothek, München Alte Pinakothek München: https://www.sammlung.pinakothek.de/en/artwork/Qlx2QpQ4Xq (updated 19.02.2020): 123l; © Photo Jonathan Bloom: 59r; © Bibliothèque nationale de France: 54; Bridgeman Images: 130t, / Art Institute of Chicago, IL, USA/© ADAGP, Paris and DACS, London 2021: 182l, / Christie's Images / © The Gluck Estate. All rights reserved, DACS 2021: 219b, / Photo © Collection Artedia © ADAGP, Paris and DACS, London 2021: 195l, / © Colin Davison / © Jenny Holzer. ARS, NY and DACS, London 2021: 203t, / © Detroit Institute of Arts, USA / Founders Society Purchase, Allen Shelden III Fund / Bridgeman Images: 168l, / Fine Art Images: 121b, / © Musée Condé, Chantilly, France: 69r, / Museum Minority Artists Purchase Fund / © Romare Bearden Foundation / VAGA at ARS, NY and DACS, London 2021: 185l, / © Museo del Templo Mayor, Mexico City, Mexico / Jean-Pierre Courau: 94l, / Philadelphia Museum of Art, Pennsylvania, / The Louise and Walter Arensberg Collection, 1950/© Association Marcel Duchamp / ADAGP, Paris and DACS, London 2021: 170l, / © Pomona College, Claremont, California / Photo: Schenck & Schenck: 181t, / © Tokyo National Museum, Japan: 112b, / Universidad Autonoma de Chapingo, Mexico / Dirk Bakker, photographer for the Detroit Institute of Arts / © Banco de México Diego Rivera Frida Kahlo Museums Trust, Mexico, D.F. / DACS 2021: 181b, / © University College of Wales, Aberystwyth, Wales / Bridgeman Images: 137tl; © Brooklyn Museum: / 86.229.5 / Gift of Evelyn A. J. Hall and John A. Friede: 145l, / 22.666 / Museum expedition 1922, Robert B. Woodward Memorial Fund: 152t; © Judy Chicago. ARS, NY and DACS, London 2021: 208l; © Jean Clottes: 16t; © CORBIS: 45l, 74l, 150l, / © Atlantide Phototravel: 84, / © Richard A. Cooke: 91r, / © epa/© 1998 Kate Rothko Prizel & Christopher Rothko, ARS, NY and DACS, London 2021: 192l, / © Michael Freeman: 87, / © Photolibrary: 144l; © DACS 2021: 185r; © Department of Antiquities, Cyprus: 37tl; © Image www.egyptmemory.com / Center for Documentation of Cultural and Natural Heritage (CULTNAT): 28r; © Fondation Louis Vuitton / Marc Domage / © The Estate of Jean-Michel Basquiat / ADAGP, Paris and DACS, London 2021: 215; Getty Images / nicolamargaret: 16br, FMGB Guggenheim Bilbao Museoa / Photo: Erika Ede, 2003 / © 2021 Calder Foundation, New York / DACS, London: 201br; Gund Gallery Collection; Gift of David Horvitz '74 and Francie Bishop Good. © Faith Ringgold / ARS, NY and DACS, London, Courtesy ACA Galleries, New York 2021: 202l; © R. Hamilton. All Rights Reserved, DACS 2021: 197tr; Collection of the Hampton University Museum, Hampton, VA: 167b; © Damien Hirst and Science Ltd. All rights reserved, DACS 2021: 194t; Photo: The Jacob and Gwendolyn Lawrence Foundation / © The Jacob and Gwendolyn Knight Lawrence Foundation, Seattle / Artists Rights Society (ARS). NY and DACS, London 2021: 177t; © Andrea Jemolo, Rome: 31; © Anish Kapoor. All Rights Reserved, DACS 2021: 200l; © Kulturhistorisk museum, Universitetet i Oslo/Truls Teigen: 65r; Kunstmuseum Basel. Donation from Professors J.J. Bachofen-Burckhardt Collection, 2015: 123r; © Photo Jürgen Liepe: 32t, 32b; Carmen Lomas GARZA / Collection of Smithsonian American Art Museum, Washington, DC.: 209l; Photo: Attilio Maranzano / © The Easton Foundation / VAGA at ARS, NY and DACS, London 2021: 201t; © Kerry James Marshall. Courtesy of the artist and Jack Shainman Gallery New York: 217t; Courtesy the artist and Metro Pictures, New York: 219t; The Metropolitan Museum of Art, New York / Purchase, The Dillon Fund Gift, 1979: 108-109, / Rogers Fund, 1998. Accession no.: 1998.66: 151r; © Photo Marc Muench: 90t; Museum of Contemporary Art San Diego. Gift of Dr and Mrs Jack M. Farris. / Artwork © Ellsworth Kelly Foundation, Courtesy Matthew Marks Gallery: 193; © Museum of Fine Arts, Boston: 93l; Museum of Modern Art, New York / © Salvador Dali, Fundació Gala-Salvador Dali, DACS 2021: 183t; Courtesy National Gallery of Art, Washington: 163br; Collection National Gallery of Art / © Estate of Joan Mitchell: 188t; © National Gallery of Australia, Canberra: 207r; National Gallery of Canada, Ottawa / Photo: NGC: 134l; Division of Cultural and Community Life, National Museum of American History, Smithsonian Institution: 177b; Photo: Nationalmuseum, Stockholm / Wikimedia Commons CC PD: 133r; © National Museums Liverpool: 55r; National Portrait Gallery, Smithsonian Institution; gift of Kate Capshaw and Steven Spielberg, Judith Kern and Kent Whealy, Tommie L. Pegues and Donald A. Capoccia, Clarence, DeLoise and Brenda Gaines, Jonathan and Nancy Lee Kemper, The Stoneridge Fund of Amy and Marc Meadows, Robert E. Meyerhoff and Rheda Becker, Catherine and Michael Podell, Mark and Cindy Aron, Lyndon J. Barrois and Janine Sherman Barrois, The Honourable John and Louise Bryson, Paul and Rose Carter, Bob and Jane Clark, Lisa R. Davis Shirley Ross Davis and Family; Alan and Lois Fern; Conrad and Constance Hipkins; Sharon and John Hoffman, Audrey M. Irmas, John Legend and Chrissy Teigen, Eileen Harris Norton, Helen Hilton Raiser, Philip and Elizabeth Ryan, Roselyne Chroman Swig, Josef Vascovitz and Lisa Goodman, Eileen Baird, Dennis and Joyce Black Family Charitable Foundation, Shelley Brazier, Aryn Drake-Lee, Andy and Teri Goodman, Randi Charno Levine and Jeffrey E. Levine, Fred M. Levin and Nancy Livingston, The Shenson Foundation, Monique Meloche Gallery, Chicago, Arthur Lewis and Hau Nguyen, Sara and John Schram, Alyssa Taubman and Robert Rothman: 217b; Photograph by Gordon Parks / Courtesy of and copyright The Gordon Parks Foundation: 175l; © The Pollock-Krasner Foundation ARS, NY and DACS, London 2021: 188b; © Gerhard Richter: 211l; © Rijksmuseum voor Volkerkunde, Leiden: 86b,105r; © Pipilotti Rist. Courtesy the artist, Hauser & Wirth and Luhring Augustine: 214t; © RMN: 23l, 23r, 40r, 41l, / Daniel Arnaudet: 140, / Gérard Blot/Christian Jean: 137tr, / René-Gabriel Ojeda: 17tr, / © Paris - Musée de l'Armée / Dist. RMN / Pascal Segrette: 136l; © Roemer und Pelizaeus Museum, Hildesheim: 28l; © Royal Academy of Arts: 137b; © 2021. Photo Scala, Florence: 20tl, 30l, 37tr, 40l, 41r, 45r, 47, 49l, 49r, 53l, 58, 68tl, 68tr, 94r, 119l, 120r, 148l, / © 2021. De Agostini Picture Library / Scala, Florence: 25, / © 2021. The Art Institute of Chicago / Art Resource NY: 164t, / © 2021 Photo Scala, Florence / Art Resource, NY / © Morgan Art Foundation Ltd / Artists Rights Society (ARS), New York, DACS, London 2021: 197b, / © 2021. Photo Scala, Florence / Art Resource / Photo 2021 Smithsonian American Art Museum / © Estate of Miriam Schapiro / ARS, NY and DACS, London 2021: 208r, / © 2021. Photo Scala, Florence / BPK, Bildagentur für Kunst, Kultur und Geschichte, Berlin: 66r, 127, 132l, / © Photo Hermann Buresch: 133l, / Photo: Sandra Steiss: 30r, / Photo Olaf M. Tessmer: 22t, 22b, / © 2021. Cameraphoto / Scala, Florence: 52, / © 2021. Christie's Images, London / Scala, Florence / © ARS, NY and DACS, London 2021: 173b, 192r, 200r, / © Georgia O'Keeffe Museum / DACS, London 2021: 154l, / © Helen Frankenthaler Foundation, Inc. / ARS, NY and DACS, London 2021: 190–191, / © Wayne Thiebaud / VAGA at ARS, NY and DACS, London 2021: 97br, / Artwork Copyright © Yue Minjun: 218r, / ©2021. Photo Fine Art Images / Heritage Images / Scala, Florence: 161l, / ©2021. Image copyright The Metropolitan Museum of Art / Art Resource / Scala, Florence: 33bl, 38l, 46, 61bl, 61br, 81t, 160, 149l, 149r, 150r, 151l, 152b, 153l, / © The Isamu Noguchi Foundation and Garden Museum / ARS, New York and DACS, London 2021: 184l, / © The Josef and Anni Albers Foundation / Artists Rights Society (ARS), New York and DACS, London 2021: 202r, / © 2021. Photo Scala, Florence, Courtesy Ministero Beni e Att. Culturali e del Turismo: 38tr, 40c, 118t, 121t, 134r, / © 2021. Image Copyright Museo Nacional del Prado © MNP / Scala, Florence: 124, / © Museum of Fine Arts, Boston. All rights reserved / Scala, Florence: 76t, © 2021. The Museum of Modern Art, New York / Scala, Florence: 164b, / © 2021. Digital image, The Museum of Modern Art, New York / Scala, Florence: 172r, 178, 198l, Scala, Florence / Digital image 2021, The Museum of Modern Art, New York / ©Vija Celmins, Courtesy Matthew Marks Gallery: 211r, / © DACS 2021: 182r, / © The Pollock-Krasner Foundation ARS, NY and DACS, London 2021: 189t, / © Man Ray 2015 Trust/DACS, London 2021: 171r, / © The Willem de Kooning Foundation / Artists Rights Society (ARS), New York and DACS, London 2021: 189b, / © 2021. Digital image, The Museum of Modern Art, New York Scala, Florence. Estate of John Hay Whitney / Succession Picasso / DACS, London 2021: 169r, / ©2021. Copyright The National Gallery, London/Scala, Florence: 118b, 122l, 130br, 131t, 139, 155t / Bought jointly by the National Gallery and National Galleries of Scotland with contributions from the Scottish Government, the National Heritage Memorial Fund, The Monument Trust, The Art Fund (with a contribution from the Wolfson Foundation), Artemis Investment Management Ltd, Binks Trust, Mr Busson on behalf of the EIM Group, Dunard Fund, The Fuserna Foundation, Gordon Getty, The Hintze Family Charitable Foundation, J. Paul Getty Jnr Charitable Trust, John Dodd, Northwood Charitable Trust, The Rothschild Foundation, Sir Siegmund Warburg's Voluntary Settlement and through public appeal, 2009. © 2021. Copyright The National Gallery, London / Scala, Florence: 126, / ©2021. Scala, Florence / Photo Art Resource / Bob Schalkwijk / © Banco de México Diego Rivera Frida Kahlo Museums Trust, Mexico, D.F. / DACS 2021: 218l, / ©2021. RMN Grand Palais / Dist. Photo SCALA, Florence: / Photographer: Christophe Fouin: 136r, / Photographer: Jean-Pierre Lagiewski. Inv.: RF.2415: 141b, / Photographer: Hervé Lewandowski: 38bc, 38br, / Stéphane Maréchalle: 135r, / © 2021. Photo Smithsonian American Art Museum / Art Resource / Scala, Florence: 176l, 176r, / ©2021. White Images / Scala, Florence: 68b, / © 2021. Digital image Whitney Museum of American Art / Licensed by Scala. Purchase, with funds from Kathryn Fleck in honor of Maxwell L. Anderson: 210t; The Solomon R. Guggenheim Foundation, New York / Photograph by David Heald / © Stephen Flavin / Artists Rights Society (ARS), New York and DACS, London 2021: 203b; Photograph © The State Hermitage Museum / Vladimir Terebenin / © Succession H. Matisse/DACS 2021: 165; © Vivan Sundaram: 180r; SuperStock/© Robert Rauschenberg Foundation / VAGA at ARS, NY and DACS 2021: 198r; © Photo © Tate: 166r, / © ADAGP, Paris and DACS, London 2021: 183b, / © 2021 The Andy Warhol Foundation for the Visual Arts, Inc. / Licensed by DACS, London 2021: 196b, / © Association Marcel Duchamp / ADAGP, Paris and DACS, London 2021: 171l, / © Estate of Roy Lichtenstein/DACS 2021: 196t, / © David Hockney: 197tl, / © the artist / © Bridget Riley 2021. All rights reserved.: 195r; © The Art Archive / Dagli Orti: 48, / National Archaeological Museum, Athens / Dagli Orti: 36br; © Tokyo National Museum: 80l, 80r; © Tropen Museum, Amsterdam: 105l; © The Trustees of the British Museum: 20b, 21t, 21b, 24l, 24r, 33tl, 64t, 64b, 79l, 111l, 113l, 144r, 148r; © Uniphoto: 77b, 78r, 106; © The University of Iowa Museum of Art, Iowa City, Iowa, The Stanley Collection, x 1990.697: 153r; © V&A Images/Victoria & Albert Museum: 104, 115; Installation view: Kara Walker, Wooster Gardens / Brent Sikkema, New York, NY, 1998 / Photo: Erma Estwick / Artwork © Kara Walker, courtesy of Sikkema Jenkins & Co., New York: 212b; The Whitney Museum of Art / © Estate of David Smith / VAGA at ARS, NY and DACS, London 2021: 201bl; ©Xu Bing Studio: 199r; © Yoshimoto Nara, courtesy Pace Gallery. Photograph by Keizo Kioku: 216r

Dear visitor,

Curating this museum for you has been one of the most rewarding and fun challenges of my career. I spent long hours thinking of how to fill these halls with art that shows beautiful and diverse histories.

There are many ways to organize a museum. I chose to split this one into three wings dedicated to different periods in human history. It's my hope that this structure helps you discover art from unique cultures and see the ways artists and styles have become more connected to each other over time.

Alas, even imaginary museums have limits! Humans have been making art for a long time, and it can't all fit in one book. That means there are places where I had to make tough decisions about which artists and artworks to include. I've tried to select a mixture of famous and lesser-known artists, taking care to highlight women and people of color. I hope you'll see some of your favorites, and discover amazing new creators you never knew.

- Ferren Gipson

ACKNOWLEDGMENTS:
Thank you to Maya Gartner and Rebecca Morrill for believing in me. Thanks to Angela Sangma Francis and Harriet Birkinshaw for your hard work and help. And, of course, to my supportive and patient husband, Tom.

Phaidon Press Inc
65 Bleecker Street,
New York, NY 10012

phaidon.com

First published 2021
© 2021 Phaidon Press Limited

The Ultimate Art Museum originates from *The Art Museum*, first published in 2011 © 2011 Phaidon Press Limited

Text set in Circular Pro, Plaak, and Sharp Slab

ISBN 978 1 83866 378 0 (US edition)
013-0721

A CIP catalog record for this book is available from the Library of Congress.

All rights reserved. No part of this publication may be reproduced, stored in a retrieval system or transmitted, in any form or by any means, electronic, mechanical, photocopying, recording or otherwise, without the written permission of Phaidon Press Limited.

Commissioning Editor: Maya Gartner
Designer: Meagan Bennett

Production Controller: Rebecca Price
Consultant Editors: AHA Editorial

Printed in Italy